CONTENTS

INTRODUCTION

There are many ways to show and share love: cooking a meal for someone, writing a poem for him or her, taking a long walk, laughing, singing, planning (or plotting), goofing off—these are all ways we show love in our lives. We show love when we live beautifully, alone or together, doing our absolute best.

These quilts are for all the ways we show and share love in our lives; they are quilts for all of our days.

In a world teeming with objects accidentally beautiful, aggressively *not* beautiful, and forgettable, quilts fall into an exceptional category: Quilts are functional *and* beautiful *and* they are made on purpose. Quilts are functional art.

A great painting is made on purpose and may function to make you feel awestruck or inspired. A piece of music may move you—it is functional in this regard. But what work of art can you literally wrap around your shoulders when you're sad?

What work of art can physically warm you? What work of art pools, folds, props up, and lies flat; can be washed, dried, cried on, and repaired; and is the first thing anyone grabs when the house is on fire? What other work of art can you make love under?

Quilts are art you can flop on top of with a dish of ice cream and your beloved. (Or just the ice cream. Or just the beloved.) These objects are workaday, household necessities and precious artifacts at the same time. Whether a person particularly *likes* a given quilt or not, virtually everyone understands and respects the value a quilt has to its owner.

Human beings love quilts because quilts are objects of love; indeed, most quilts are made and given to someone as a gift. Just as love is not selfish, neither are quilters. A quilt is a physical manifestation of the sentiment, "You are cared for. I want you to be warm and dry." If you're really lucky, a quilt can mean, "Without question, I love you."

NOTES ON THIS BOOK

BIG, BIGGER, BIGGEST

Quilters are impatient people.

To a nonquilter, this seems almost laughably wrong. Aren't quilters gentle, steady folk, content to stitch all afternoon in a rocking chair? Not only is this impression incorrect with regard to quilters in the past—early American quilters hardly had leisure time—it's untrue today. Dedicated quilters are foot-tappers, forever on the lookout for ways to get quilts done more quickly and efficiently for one simple reason: we want to make our next quilt as soon as possible.

Because of this impatience (we think of it as passion), and because we're awfully busy otherwise, there is significant interest in what's called the small project. Wallhangings, pillows, baby quilts, and table runners are all small sewing projects that satisfy a quilter's innate impatience; many of these projects can be completed in a single day.

The quilts in this book … not so much. These quilts are big. Depending on how frequently you get to your sewing machine, these quilts may take you some time to complete. Unless you know something I don't, they will stubbornly refuse to be finished in a day.

These quilts are designed for beds, and your bed is probably queen- or king-size. A queen-size mattress in the United States measures approximately 60″ × 80″, a king-size, 76″ × 80″. Quilts are meant to drape over a bed, not just sit on top of it, so a quilt for an adult-sized bed needs to measure anywhere from 88″ × 90″ to 90″ × 100″ or bigger, depending on the size of the people who will use it.

For those who want a quick quilt fix, this book will make an excellent coaster. But I urge even the most impatient of quilters to consider taking on a large quilt. The quilts that take our breath away at shows and exhibits are the big ones. In terms of color and pattern, what's good in a small quilt is stunning in a big one. When you see a bedroom with a generous quilt on the bed, you marvel and coo—scale is powerful. It's also practical. Big quilts are body-sized, comfort-sized. No one wants their feet sticking out the bottom of the covers. Besides, you can't make love under a table topper.

SCRAP LOVE

Aside from being large, the quilts in this book can be classified as scrap quilts—they are made from many different fabrics.

There are as many different kinds of quilts in the world as there are quilters, including some people who make quilts using approximately four to six fabrics, frequently from a single line within a manufacturer's collection. There is nothing wrong with this approach. In fact, there are benefits to making quilts with only a handful of fabrics from a new line—it's faster, you're unlikely to have color or contrast surprises, and you're sure to be on trend.

Scrap quilts, at least the way I approach them, are a different animal. There will always be surprises, accidents, and problems to solve. It cannot be denied: Making extremely scrappy quilts takes more time than making quilts with a small number of fabrics. Notwithstanding the time it takes to select the scraps themselves (this will take some significantly longer than others), you'll have to iron, cut, and sort or otherwise organize every piece.

But the extra work is worth it. Intelligently scrappy quilts have a depth and a beauty hard to achieve with a six-fabric quilt. The six-fabric quilt will have its charm, but I like dozens and dozens of fabrics playing together. There's a surprise in every block. Every quilt becomes a charm quilt; every quilt is head-slappingly unique. This is a great joy for a quilter and can assuage the pain of early arthritis brought on by hours at the cutting mat.

Whenever I get antsy about finishing my cutting, whenever I start feeling "done" with a quilt before I've finished joining rows, I stop and ask myself why I'm making the quilt in the first place. You might ask yourself the same thing. Hopefully, our goal is the same: We want to create a functional object of beauty and be proud of an accomplishment. Hopefully, we make quilts because we want to show someone love—and that person might be you, yourself. So turn on the radio and enjoy the scrap quilt process. Yes, it takes a long time to make a big scrap quilt, but so what?

Do you have something better to do?

HOW THIS BOOK IS STRUCTURED

In the first few chapters, a bit of theory and practice are presented to help place these quilts in context while offering fundamental process information.

By examining the way I approach quilt design, you will hopefully be able to analyze your own methods and preferences and perhaps adopt some new ideas. By looking at why the quilts we make today look the way they do, you may be inspired to take your work in an entirely new direction, which would be great. In quiltmaking, as in life, innovation, creativity, and exploration are concepts to be championed and supported.

Construction notes and basic instructions will help you in the creation of your quilt. I have been taught that best practices in patchwork and quilting are encouraged not because quilters are perfectionist taskmasters but because when you sew accurately, sewing is more enjoyable. Fudging a bit here means you'll have to fudge a bit there, and on and on until there is woe and pans of fudge. Strive for accurate, tidy patchwork and you'll avoid a great deal of suffering.

You could, theoretically, make a quilt from start to finish using only this book as your guide, but that is only recommended if you live 3,000 miles from everywhere and are still churning your own butter. Take advantage of the quilt world and all it has to teach you! Take classes. Watch videos online. Learn from a mentor. However and wherever you can get instruction in your new passion, get it. You'll learn far more than could be wrangled into the pages of this slender book.

MAKE IT YOURS

I sincerely hope that you find this book to be a source of inspiration and a point of departure. I feel a singular excitement when I see a quilt that I love and fantasize about my version of it. If I see a Feathered Star in red and white, I'm giddy when considering the possibilities: What if it were done in black and pink? What might it look like in scrappy blues? What if I made the stars smaller and took the border away?

However you make your versions, even if they are nearly identical to the quilts you see on these pages, I hope you enjoy every stitch, every sweet hour of the process.

A BRIEF HISTORY OF QUILTMAKING

In the beginning, women in America made quilts out of necessity. It was simple: Members of their family were cold. They first made them with fabric scraps and material they repurposed; later, they made them out of an abundance of fabric suddenly available thanks to the Industrial Revolution. But whether material was scarce or in surplus, these early quiltmakers *didn't have to make these covers beautiful*. Any patched blanket would do the job of covering their loved ones. American patchworkers innovated and elevated the making of "blankets" into art—into quilts.

Most of their stitched designs were built with or around quilt blocks, combined units of patchwork that typically were a perfect square. Women designed these blocks without the aid of computers or fancy drafting tools and gave them names: Churn Dash, Sawtooth Star, Bird of Paradise, Monkey Wrench, Flower Basket, and hundreds if not thousands of others. Blocks are timeless examples of good design. The dimensions of traditional quilt blocks are balanced and geometric; when the blocks are coupled or paired with different blocks, one instantly understands how limitless the design possibilities truly are. Intricate borders and simple ones, curved seams, appliqué, repeating patterns, interlocking pieces—these were all in the repertoire of the "traditional" quilter and remain a treasure trove of inspiration and instruction for quilters of all styles today.

The colors used in antique quilts remain sophisticated. Colors like poison green, cheddar, antimony orange, and turkey red in quilts of the nineteenth century all feel fresh, even edgy. The muted grays and blacks seem "modern." In some ways, quiltmaking these days is too easy. The hardest work has been done; we're standing on the shoulders of giants.

> Love many things, for therein lies the true strength, and whosoever loves much performs much, and can accomplish much, and what is done in love is done well.
>
> VINCENT VAN GOGH

WHAT HAS BEEN DONE WILL BE DONE AGAIN

As quilts and quiltmaking increased in popularity throughout the 1980s and 1990s, different styles emerged and camps were formed. There were quilters who left traditional forms behind and struck out to make art or studio quilts. These quilters embellished fabric, painted it, or worked in metal, clay, beads, and all manner of textures to create quilts that hung on gallery walls, never to touch a mattress.

For those who still wanted quilts for the home, myriad color palettes and new techniques emerged around the same time; in the late 1980s a marked difference developed between the creations of the "traditional" quilter and the "contemporary" one. A contemporary look made use of bright batiks and saturated jewel tones, and frequently employed embroidery or metallic thread; paper piecing was (and continues to be) a popular method for so-called contemporary quilters who wish to create new shapes in their quilts.

The first Modern Quilt Guild, formed in Los Angeles in 2009, promoted another shift in the quilt world. Pictures of quilts making use of negative space, improvisational piecing techniques, and almost entirely solid (nonprinted) cotton were being shared online, with rapid, ravenous interest via blogs and photo-sharing sites. Modern guilds popped up across the country, and just as with the art quilters and the contemporary quilters before them, a division emerged early on between the traditional and modern camps.

I have no doubt that in my lifetime we will see at least one more shift, probably two, in the styles, mode, and direction of quiltmaking in America. The only threat to the health of the quilt world is rejection of the new and impatience with or disdain for the beginner. These are unpardonable sins. We must embrace and support the beginner quilter or lose her—and the art itself—for good.

As my mother says, "It doesn't matter what kind of quilts people are making, as long as people are making quilts."

I, QUILTER

I design around traditional blocks and sew by standard construction methods. Does that make me a traditional quilter? I am drawn to a twenty-first-century color palette and am inspired by fashion runways and fine art—perhaps that makes me "modern." I don't think it matters. I'm a quilter. I make the quilts that please me; it's up to other people to put labels on them. My hope is that every quilter can feel free to make the quilts she wants to make, hang the categories.

FABRIC

SCRAP QUILTS IN THE TWENTY-FIRST CENTURY

No matter what kind of quilts you make, you're in luck: The quilt world offers up thousands of distinct fabrics each year. Some of these fabrics are continually popular and reproduced—red and white polka dots, solid black, and so on. Some fabrics are reprints or older fabrics popular enough to be brought back to market. The vast majority of fabric produced each year, however, is brand new.

The mountains of cotton broadcloth produced for quilting today greatly influence the way our quilts look. Any color or print you can dream up probably exists; if it doesn't, you can design and print your own fabric digitally on demand. Naturally, there's plenty of fabric you will decide *not* to include in any quilt, ever, but to me, it only makes sense to plumb the immeasurable depths of fabric options available. For me, making a quilt with just a handful of fabrics feels limited. The world of fabric has grown and evolved. As a quilter quilting in the twenty-first century, I want to evolve along with it.

FABRIC FOR BACKINGS

Another positive result of having so much fabric available in the world is watching your stash and scrap bin grow without even trying. If you make quilts with any regularity, you're going to have material left over. Most patterns call for a tad extra fabric in case you make a mistake; if you don't, good on you—you've got fabric for another project. Your stash will also grow because you will buy fabric. Over and over and over again, you will buy fabric because it is very, very, very fun.

A perfect place to use some of this treasured fabric is on the back of your quilt. The backs of quilts in this book are pictured just to show you what I did; directions aren't given because I didn't give myself much direction when I made them.

THE 1,000 IDEAS THEORY

Every fabric on the market is the embodiment of an idea a designer had. It's the result of a complex production process. Think of the journey fabric took to get to your warm, snuggly bed: its design went from an artist's mind to paper or computer, from image to engraving plate or series of digital 0's and 1's, from data to mill, from mill to bolt, bolt to shop, shop to you, you to quilt.

When I'm under a quilt that has been constructed from dozens and dozens of scraps I personally selected from the zillions of fabrics out there, my quilt is blanketing me in ideas; I'm sleeping under intricate, careful processes, under sophisticated intelligence and love itself.

Here's the only rule you need: If you intend to quilt your quilt via longarm, the back of your quilt must be 6″–10″ bigger on all sides than the top of the quilt itself. For domestic sewing machines, 4″ is a good minimum.

That's it. After that, do whatever you like. What a waste to view a quilt back as obligatory or allow it to always be plain. I see each back like the B-side of a single or an LP (remember those?)—something special, unique, and almost as cool as the A-side. It's a bonus, an extra, a surprise.

A good friend of mine likes making the backs of her quilts more than the fronts. "I get to play, let loose," she says. I've been encouraging her to make the back first, and then stick a back on that.

WHY QUILTS ARE COTTON

It's common for people to become interested in quiltmaking because they have a pile of Grandma's dresses, Dad's neckties, or their own college debate team T-shirts that they want to turn into something less depressing. This is a fine reason to want to sit down at a sewing machine, but these can be rather advanced projects. This is due to the nature of the materials (knit, lace, silk, and so on), which often need to be stabilized and/or sewn with specialty thread.

Most quilts today are made with 100% cotton broadcloth. If you're approaching quilting for the first time, I highly recommend using this material.

One-hundred percent cotton broadcloth is a densely woven, extremely sturdy, soft cotton fabric. It's the primary material quilt fabric manufacturers make and almost exclusively what quilt shops sell.

We use this material because it has a good hand, it needles well, and it's strong enough to be used and washed again and again. There are different levels of quality in 100% cotton broadcloth. Buy the best you can afford. Good cotton broadcloth is generally 44″–45″ wide. The projects in this book are based on 42″ of usable width.

A NOTE ON LINEN

There is a fabric called "quiltmaker's linen" that I like very much. This thick linen fabric plays well with regular cotton broadcloth and has a lovely texture. You will see this fabric show up in several of the quilts in this book.

THE PREWASH QUESTION

I do not prewash my fabric before I cut it up. Here's why:

- Most fabric comes preshrunk.
- Quality fabric will not bleed when washed.
- The amount of sizing solution used on fabric is nominal.
- I don't want to do more laundry.
- Smoothing yards and yards of wrinkly fabric for hours at the ironing board? No. Way.

Here are reasons why some people prewash:

- They like the extra softness that comes with washing.
- They may have sensitivity to fabric sizing used in manufacturing.
- They don't want to take any chances with dye bleed.
- They don't mind laundry.

You can decide which side you're on, but whatever you choose, consistency is key. If you pre-wash some fabric but not all of it, there may be unpleasant puckering or general unevenness when you wash your quilt; the prewashed fabric will launder differently than the fabric that is being washed for the first time.

If I were making a white and red quilt, I would probably prewash my fabrics. Red dye is prone to bleeding (even the good stuff), and next to snow white it could be tragic. Outside of a project like that, however, I find pre-washing to be an unnecessary step. When I get fabric home, I make a beeline for the cutting mat. So far, I have not regretted working with fabric directly off the bolt, unwashed.

SOLIDS

Solids began to experience renewed popularity with the arrival of Modern Quilt Guild groups; before that, all-solid fabrics were the stars of Amish quilts and other antique quilts from the late nineteenth and early twentieth centuries.

There are many reasons for the solid revolution, none definitive. Using solids in quilts may have been a response to the busy patterns in the fabric of years prior. It might have simply been a micro-trend that caught on and stuck. It surely reflects an affinity for the quilts of Gee's Bend, Alabama, which toured the country in an exhibit in the 1990s, which received extensive media coverage.

I believe the strongest quilts have a bit of solid and a bit of print in them. I make intensely scrappy quilts but slow down that scrappiness with a measure of consistent, solid color. Solids and scraps are perfect foils. All-solid quilts hold little interest for me (too flat), as do 100% scrappy quilts (too chaotic). Quilts are like dogs: the smartest, strongest ones are usually mixed breeds.

THE DRESS TEST

With so many choices, it can be difficult selecting fabrics for your project. If you've been making quilts for a long time, you may have developed a palette: you know you prefer a softer white over a brighter one, you rarely use brick red, every quilt seems to contain some shade of mango, and so on. This helps winnow down a few bolts, but you're still facing an unsettling number of choices.

PALETTE:

the range of colors used by a particular quilter or in a particular quilt

I have developed a method for fabric selection in my quilts I call the "Dress Test." If you've ever shopped for clothes, you can understand the thinking behind this method; if you *love* shopping for clothes as much as I do, you may decide to use the method yourself.

When a particular fabric catches my eye in a quilt shop or on a website, I ask myself, "Would I wear a dress made of this?" The question is rhetorical; what I'm examining is the print, not the cotton itself. I'm essentially asking, "Would I wear this pattern on my body?"

If the answer is yes—and there are degrees of this (see Degrees of "Yes," at right)—then I know that fabric will be at home in any quilt I make. I rarely shop for a particular project; I buy fabric liberally and keep my stash robust so that when inspiration arrives I have plenty to work with. Because each fabric in my stash has passed the Dress Test, I'm stocked entirely with fabric that I don't just "like," but adore. Legendary decorative artist William Morris said, "Have nothing in your home that you don't know to be useful or believe to be beautiful." Whether I'm buying a can opener, a sofa, or a fat quarter, if I don't think it's going to be useful or if I don't think it's beautiful, it will not come home with me. I have a lot of fabric, but Morris' suggestion actually keeps my stash from getting out of control—and I'm in love with every yard.

This method works for me because I have a deep love for fashion. For those who don't care about fashion, my Dress Test might not work, which is fine; there are lots of ways to find your palette. The point is, buy fabric you love and want to work with. As you make more and more quilts, this palette will emerge. Enjoy the discovery.

DEGREES OF "YES"

A dress for sure:
This is a fabric that you want to live in. Buy at least 4 yards.

Definitely a blouse:
You love it. Buy 2 yards.

Ooh, tote bag:
Get a half-yard cut or several fat quarters.

The perfect scarf:
Get scraps, remnants, or fat quarters.

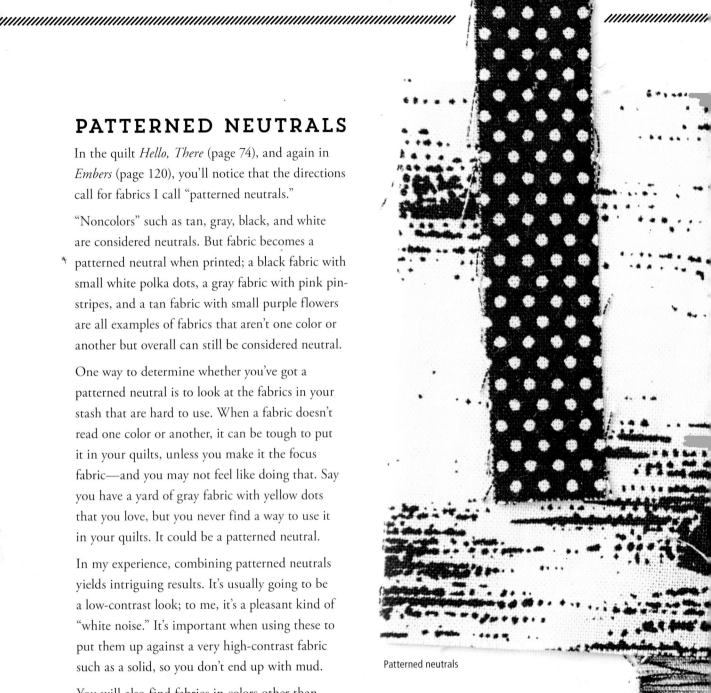

PATTERNED NEUTRALS

In the quilt *Hello, There* (page 74), and again in *Embers* (page 120), you'll notice that the directions call for fabrics I call "patterned neutrals."

"Noncolors" such as tan, gray, black, and white are considered neutrals. But fabric becomes a patterned neutral when printed; a black fabric with small white polka dots, a gray fabric with pink pinstripes, and a tan fabric with small purple flowers are all examples of fabrics that aren't one color or another but overall can still be considered neutral.

One way to determine whether you've got a patterned neutral is to look at the fabrics in your stash that are hard to use. When a fabric doesn't read one color or another, it can be tough to put it in your quilts, unless you make it the focus fabric—and you may not feel like doing that. Say you have a yard of gray fabric with yellow dots that you love, but you never find a way to use it in your quilts. It could be a patterned neutral.

In my experience, combining patterned neutrals yields intriguing results. It's usually going to be a low-contrast look; to me, it's a pleasant kind of "white noise." It's important when using these to put them up against a very high-contrast fabric such as a solid, so you don't end up with mud.

You will also find fabrics in colors other than neutral tans, grays, and so on but could still be used as patterned neutrals—in *My Dear* (page 96), I consider the busy flower prints to be patterned neutrals even though they are within the purple and blue family.

Patterned neutrals

Combining patterned neutrals
yields intriguing results.

DESIGN
FUNDAMENTALS

While it is true that beauty is subjective, that tastes vary and styles come and go, a quilt can be considered functional art when two primary elements of design are working in harmony: pattern and color.

Pattern is the arrangement or sequence of the pieces of the quilt top—block selection, scale, dimensions, border choices, appliqué shape and placement if used, and so on. To perceive pattern, there must be contrast.

When speaking of **color** in quilts, we're talking about **fabric.** Selecting the fabric to be used in a quilt is one of the greatest pleasures of the process. It can also be daunting, because there are so many fabrics to choose from, and after you sew everything together and quilt your quilt, those choices are permanent. If you decide you don't like your fabrics after all, you'll have to make another quilt. There are worse problems to have.

Understanding the fundamentals of good design will serve you well as you embark on a quilt, whether you've made dozens of them or zero. The following is a brief survey well worth your time, even if you don't consider yourself a designer—yet.

There is no time for cut-and-dried monotony. There is time for work. And time for love. That leaves no other time.

COCO CHANEL

CONTRAST

A light blue against a deep red in a Churn Dash block yields a high-contrast block. A light blue against a slightly darker blue yields a low-contrast block.

High contrast

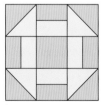
Low contrast

Contrast is always relative. Always. Black and white used together are high contrast. Black and slate gray used together? Medium contrast. Black and deep charcoal used together? Low contrast. Contrast can be hard to get the hang of when you're a beginner quilter; even experienced quilters have unhappy accidents from time to time as a result of contrast issues. (Ask me how I know.)

 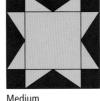 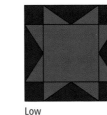

High   Medium   Low

The lesson here: You must learn to *read* fabric. To read a fabric means to see how it will appear from a distance of six feet or more. That is an unscientific calculation, but it feels about right to most quilters. Learning how fabric reads is one of the most valuable skills a quilter can possess.

Up close, a black and charcoal Star block looks like it was made with two different fabrics—and it was. But stand back six feet and suddenly you've lost the block—it will just read dark, and your cute Star block will appear as a solid dark square. This is a problem if you want your piecing to show, as most people do. However, low-contrast blocks can be used to great effect. Check out *Night Sky* (page 112). The low-contrast, black-on-black blocks serve as a kind of textural background so that the sprinkling of high-contrast blocks jump out and move the eye around.

Low- or high-contrast choices aren't good or bad; they just create different effects. Once you understand them, you can make them work for you.

HUE AND VALUE

Hue is nothing more (or less) than the color of a fabric. **Value** is the relative degree of lightness or darkness of that color. At right, the *hue* is hot pink; the *value* is medium.

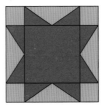

Hue is hot pink. Value is medium.

Hue is fairly straightforward. Though one person's hot pink is another person's magenta, color or hue is fairly standardized and basically fixed. New Jersey–based Pantone LLC sets global standards for the colors we use in everything from paper to fabric to cars. A great tool for any designer in any medium, including yours, is a Pantone color book (Resources, page 127).

But as with contrast, **the value of colors is also always relative**. Take the Star block, for example. If you keep it pink but change the value (the lightness or darkness) of the pinks, you get very different looks. As you can imagine, there are infinite varieties when you're talking value.

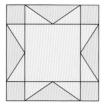 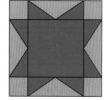

Light pink   Medium pink   Dark pink

Various values of pink

SCALE

Scale is the size of something and pertains to both fabric and overall design.

SCALE IN FABRIC

In fabric, scale is the size of the print. Prints can be effectively separated into two categories: large-scale and small-scale.

> **NOTE**
> You could parse out medium-scale prints, but this makes things unnecessarily complicated. If it works for you to separate prints into additional categories, feel free to do so; for now, we'll just call them large- or small-scale and leave it at that.

A **large-scale** print is any fabric printed with a design that measures 3″ or bigger before it repeats. A **small-scale** print is anything that measures smaller than that. A small-scale print can be as

small as a pin dot and may read as a solid, even up close.

The fabrics used in the quilt tops in this book are small-scale prints, almost without exception. I gravitate toward small-scale prints because I find the delicacy and fineness of them immensely satisfying. Maybe it's because I get credit for an attention to detail that I had nothing to do with.

Small-scale prints don't yield surprises when you cut them up. A 2″ × 2″ square of a small print

Large-scale print   Small-scale print

reads the same as a 4″ × 4″ square, a 10″ × 12″ rectangle, or a 2-yard cut of the same fabric. When a large-scale print is cut into lots of small pieces, consistency vanishes. Say you've got a fabric printed with large leaves and branches with pink flowers, all set against light blue. When you cut this print into 2″ × 2″ squares, you'll end up with some squares made up of only pink, some just blue, and some with shades of green, and so on. Smaller pieces than that will vary further still. This can cause problems if you don't know to watch for it.

SCALE:
the relative size of something

Large-scale print

2½″ × 2½″ cut

Several 1½″ × 1½″ cuts

Just as contrast choices aren't good or bad, neither are scale choices. It pays to understand them, that's all. For me, large-scale prints have a perfect home: on the back. They can shine, and I can enjoy them in all their big, splashy glory. (For my approach to making backings, see Fabric for Backings, page 12.)

The first block might be beautiful to someone, but it's tough to see the patchwork, and the integrity of the fabric is compromised. It can be argued, therefore, that it is less successful than the block on the right, which uses a contrasting fabric to highlight the patchwork. With 2″ × 2″ finished squares, small-scale prints have advantages.

SCALE IN OVERALL DESIGN

Scale doesn't just pertain to fabric. Quilt blocks have their own scale, too. Take a look at *Herzog* (page 90). Those big X's are really just giant versions of a block called Thousand Waves. Change the size of a block significantly and you've got a very different quilt.

A quilt's overall dimensions represent a design choice as well. Louis Sullivan, the great American architect, pointed out that "form follows function." So it is with quilts. Consider the difference between a baby quilt and a king-size one. The *function* of both is to keep someone warm. But these quilts will be *formed* very differently, since one quilt is for a little baby and the other one is for a full-grown ... king? You see what I mean.

SELECTING FABRICS FOR A QUILT

You've got gorgeous fabrics in your stash (see Dress Test, page 15). So, how do you use this knowledge of pattern and color now that it's really time to get down to business? I recommend that you audition fabrics before you start cutting—place the fabrics you want to use next to or on top of each other to see how contrast, hue, and value are working (or not working) together. Look at how the colors and patterns read. If you switch out one fabric for another, perhaps of a different scale, value, or color, do you like it better? Does it pop? Does it disappear? It can be frustrating when you love fabrics that don't actually work together. Don't despair—there are more quilts to make! You'll find a home for any fabric you love eventually, so do what's best for the quilt you're making now.

ROGUE BLOCKS

Flip through any book of antique quilts or see a show of vintage pieces and you will find quilts that look one way three-quarters of the way down and then look a little different. Perhaps the quiltmaker threw a color or design curveball because she was a genius, but interruptions or "maverick moments" in quilts often happened because the quiltmaker simply ran out of fabric. She made do, and this veering off, this unexpected divergence, is beautiful.

Rogue blocks are blocks that diverge from the general color repetition in a quilt. I make them happen on purpose. I like an errant moment in a quilt, an unexpected block. It's a little weird, a little playful, a bit mysterious. And it's a scam, because I am hardly working with scarce material. I incorporate rogue or maverick blocks because I like the way they look.

Look at *Night Sky* (page 112). The red blocks are rogue blocks. In *Northbound* (page 40), there's a single

bright yellow set of Flying Geese: that's a rogue. Rogue patches or blocks draw the eye to a single point in the quilt—they're disruptive. You notice the imperfection, and all of a sudden the whole is more perfect.

The great *Vogue* editor Diana Vreeland once said: "Vulgarity is a very important ingredient in life. I'm a great believer in vulgarity—if it's got vitality. A little bad taste is like a nice splash of paprika. We all need a splash of bad taste—it's hearty, it's healthy, it's physical. I think we could use more of it. No taste is what I'm against."

Do what you want in your quilts. Create intrigue by adding a spot of vulgarity, keep things strict, or write your own rules. It's your quilt. I encourage you to see each quilt you make, whatever you do, as an opportunity for a secret or a story—in each quilt, create a message in a bottle.

CONSTRUCTION BASICS

THE PATCHWORK QUARTET:
CUTTING, SEWING, PRESSING, AND RIPPING

To make patchwork, you must do three things to fabric: cut, sew, and press. A student of mine once pointed out that everyone has to rip out a seam eventually, so really, making patchwork is four things: cutting, sewing, pressing, and ripping. There was much nodding of heads.

Setting aside mistakes for now, the first three elements have been used to make patchwork for hundreds of years. You first cut pieces. Then you sew them together. Pressing embeds the stitch and both opens and flattens the fabric. The three steps must be present to create patchwork. If you've got problems with what you're making, there's something wrong in one of these three areas.

In this chapter you'll find cutting, sewing, and pressing basics. We'll take a brief look at quilting the quilt and, yes, Virginia, how to properly rip out a seam.

NOTE

For every method you learn in quiltmaking, there are other methods that will work just as well. Take classes, experiment, fail, invent, and run from anyone who claims her method for this or that technique the only right or true one. Most of us sew the way our teacher(s) sewed, and some of us are totally self-taught; in either case, practices are rarely standardized. Keep an open mind and remember: Accuracy is encouraged—not to be fussy, but to help you more fully enjoy this rewarding art form.

Pleasure in the job puts perfection in the work.

ARISTOTLE

CUTTING

Like most quilters I know, I use the rotary cutting system to cut pieces for my quilts. In addition to being faster than cutting pieces by hand, rotary cutting, when done correctly, is more likely to yield accurate pieces. This is because of the thinness of the cutter blade and the super-calibrated ruler that attends it. There are growing numbers of die-cutting aficionados and those who may prefer to snip by hand; to each his own.

ROTARY CUTTING RULES

- Close or cover the blade when you're not using your cutter.

- Keep rotary cutters far away from kids.

- Cut away from yourself, never toward.

- Use a safety glove.

When cutting fabric for quilts, you will often be cutting strips. To do this, square off the end of the fabric before measuring or cutting anything.

1. Fold the fabric selvage to selvage, adjusting so there is no diagonal wrinkle.

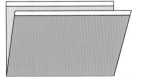

Fold fabric selvage to selvage for cutting.

THE MIGHTY FONS & PORTER

Within the quilt world, I have a *"rawther"* famous mother, Marianne Fons. She and Liz Porter, her business partner for more than 25 years, played more than a supporting role in building the quilt industry as we know it. Educators, authors, engineers, publishers, television hosts, and, of course, master quilters—Mom and Liz are two people every quilter either knows about or will know about as soon as she puts a thimble into the craft. They're legendary women, and I have the good fortune to have been raised by one of them.

In this book, I use several Fons & Porter tools. One of the things that made Fons & Porter so insanely popular with quilters everywhere was their ability to make quilting more fun by making it easier. Books such as *The Quilter's Complete Guide* and the *Love of Quilting* magazine and TV show are invaluable resources, and many of the rulers and notions Fons & Porter created are standard in many quilters' toolkits.

As with methods, though, tools can be interchanged or eliminated entirely. You can use a template if you don't want to buy a special ruler, you can draw a line with a regular pencil instead of a ceramic one, and so on. But when I suggest a Fons & Porter tool in this book, I sincerely believe it's the best way to get the job done. Hi, Mom!

2. Using the lines on the mat or a ruled square, align the fabric fold along one line. Bring a longer cutting ruler perpendicular to the mat line or the ruled square. If you have used a ruled square, move that away and use the rotary cutter to slice the folded fabric along the edge of the ruler.

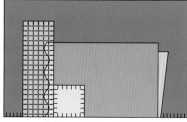

Square up fabric.

3. Cut strips along the grain of the fabric. (See Grain, Bias, and the Pop Test, next page, for information on grain and bias and how to make sure you're cutting with the grain when you want to be.) Check the fabric periodically to make sure everything is squared up properly and that the strips are being cut accurately. Cut with commitment, making sure to go through all the layers.

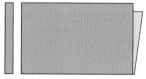

Cut strips with commitment.

4. Now that you have strips, you can continue to cut triangles or squares as needed. Take the strip, turn it a quarter-turn, and then subcut what you need.

TIME FOR A CHANGE?

How often to change the blade on your rotary cutter? It depends how much you cut. Let's say you're making every single quilt in this book. Great! Be sure to have a few extra blades on hand, and change the blade whenever you notice it is not cutting cleanly. It will make the job so much easier.

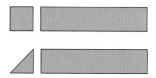

Subcut strips as needed.

GRAIN, BIAS, AND THE POP TEST

Cotton fabric is a woven textile. Threads on huge looms cross each other, creating warp and weft. Warp threads run north and south; weft threads go east and west.

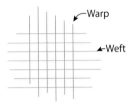

Warp threads run north and south, or up and down; weft threads run east and west, or right and left.

When you cut along the "grain" or the "straight of grain," it means you're cutting *with* the warp or weft threads. When you cut this way, you maintain the integrity of the weave.

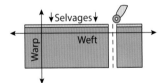

Cutting along straight of grain

When you cut on a diagonal across the weave, you're cutting on the *bias*. You compromise the weave of the fabric, and now you have a vulnerable edge—there's nothing to stop pieces with a bias edge from unraveling or stretching, unless you stabilize them.

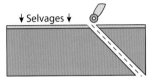

Bias cutting across weave

All the instructions in this book call for cutting triangles from strips (or using paper piecing), so you won't have to worry about bias edges in the wrong places if you follow the previous instructions. Always place the selvage of the yardage at the top of the cutting mat and the strips will be cut on the straight of grain.

Ah, but we're working with so many scraps, and not every scrap has a selvage to go by. I recommend the pop test.

Grasp the fabric so that you have about an inch between your fingers. Give the scrap a firm tug. If you hear (and feel) a sturdy little "pop!" you've found a straight-of-grain side. If what you tug makes no sound and gives easily or stretches a lot, that's bias. Place the "pop" side across the top of the cutting mat and cut the strips accordingly.

SEWING

Patchwork quilts are constructed by sewing together smaller pieces to make larger units, then joining those sections into blocks. Blocks are then joined into rows, and rows are joined to complete the top.

Quilters use a ¼″ seam allowance in patchwork because it's small enough to stay out of the way yet strong enough to hold a quilt together. But, before you sew any pieces together, arrange the pieces for a block right side up, as you see in the instructions. Then place them right sides or "pretty sides" together and sew the seam.

Arranging the blocks before you sew is a good way to see that the fabrics you've chosen are going to work (see Selecting Fabrics for a Quilt, page 23) and that you've got all the pieces you need.

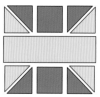
Block layout—presewing

Take a Seam Test

How do you know your ¼″ seam is correct? Do a standard seam test. Cut 2 squares 3″ × 3″. Put the pretty sides together and sew the seam. Press the seam with the iron to set it, then open up the piece and press the seams to one side (for pressing guidelines, see Pressing, page 30). Using a ruler, measure across the joined squares. If they don't measure exactly 5½″ across, adjust accordingly as described in Fixing Your Seam (next column).

Fixing Your Seam

Most of the time, an inaccurate seam allowance is due to user error, not because something is wrong with your machine. First, assess your presser foot. I use a patchwork foot on my machine, which is a foot with a little guide on the side that gives me a ¼″ seam every time if I keep my fabric up against it. It's as close to foolproof as it gets.

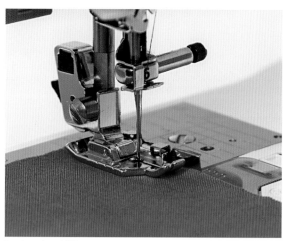
Patchwork or ¼″ foot

If you don't have a patchwork foot, you're probably going by a line etched into the throat plate or a line on the plastic apron of the machine. If your seam is off, it may be that you're putting the fabric too far to one side of these guides. It's also possible that the needle position may be in a funky place. This is when you get your manual out and make sure the needle is coming down where you want it.

If you don't have a patchwork foot, try this:

1. Lift the presser foot and make sure the needle is all the way up.

2. Carefully place a rotary cutting ruler under the presser foot, as though you are about to sew your ruler. (Don't.)

3. With your right hand on the hand wheel, gently bring the needle down onto the ruler, adjusting the ruler with your left hand to make the needle come smack down onto the ¼″ mark.

4. Lower the presser foot. Your ruler should stay right there in place.

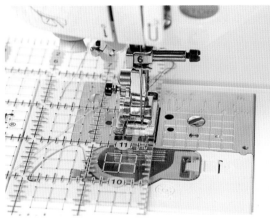
Align ruler so needle is exactly at ¼″ mark.

5. Using a long piece of painter's tape (the blue kind that doesn't leave goo), carefully place the tape onto the sewing machine's bed, using the right side of the ruler as your guide. Run the tape right off the end of the machine apron and tear off the excess.

Use painter's tape to mark ¼″.

6. When you have the tape down, raise the needle and remove the ruler. If you've been careful, you should now have an excellent ¼″ guide; just keep the right edge of your piecing running right at that line.

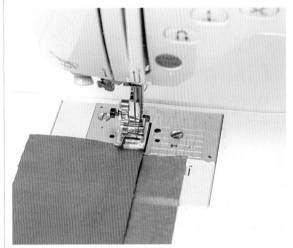
¼″ seam guide, tape method

TIP

Your sewing machine's user guide is a beautiful thing. You can throw away the little book that comes with your toaster oven, but keep your sewing machine manual for as long as you have your machine, as it will give you ideas and help you when you have issues. Many sewing machine guides will suggest still other ways for you to check seam accuracy.

Chain Piecing

Because the quilts in this book have many blocks with many pieces, you'll be doing a lot of chain piecing—sewing together pieces one after another without cutting the thread between them. Yes, chains can get extremely long.

The project instructions in this book don't specifically say to chain piece this or that, but anytime you are stitching a number of pieces in the same way, chain piecing is your friend.

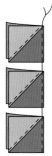

Chain piecing

Once you've run out of pieces to chain, cut the chain from your machine. Now you'll snip apart the pieces. I like to do this in a skirt—I'll explain. Go to a different chair or space in the room with your snips (small scissors) and a bowl. Put the long chain to one side and clip the threads and any visible dog-ears into your lap. Put the snipped units into the bowl.

Once you've snipped apart the chain and trimmed the threads, take your lapful of thread and bits of fabric and "foof" it outside for birds to use in their nests. Take the units to your pressing surface and press accordingly.

PRESSING

Some people hate "the pressing part" because when they look at an ironing board, they think of ironing shirts. But pressing is my favorite of the three patchwork steps because applying heat to the fabric to set the seam and then opening up each piece is so rewarding. It's like Christmas! And the good news is that *ironing* is precisely what you *don't* want to do in patchwork—*pressing* is what's fun.

Ironing is the act of using pressure to smooth fabric this way and that. When we need to get wrinkles out of an Oxford shirt, we iron. *Pressing* is different; when we press, we don't want to smooth out or smoosh our fabric around. It's truly a press, more like stamping and holding the heat to your fabric with the hot iron.

STEAM OR NO STEAM?

Steam is a fickle friend to a quilter. As you hopefully know and accept by now, every quilter has her own methods in the sewing room, and steam use is one of those areas where habits differ. However, there are a few truths about steam that are important to understand before you select your preference.

> **A TIP FROM THE PROS**
> My mother is a lifelong, professional quilter who is frequently asked about her steam preference. "I do use steam when I press," she says, "until my iron runs out of water. Then I don't." Take it from the pros.

Moisture helps "set" your piecing because when the water hits the fabric, the fibers in the cotton swell ever so slightly. When the iron's intense heat comes down on the fabric, those fibers shrink up again—only now they're tighter. The fabric "grips" the thread, and vice versa, which yields strong and secure piecing. I have also been told that the moisture/heat mix "embeds" the stitch into the fabric. This makes sense.

But too much moisture followed by heat can wreak havoc on fabric. (I told you steam was a fickle friend.) If you hit the steam button so that your fabric isn't lightly moistened but actually wet, you can grossly misshape your piecing when you press it with the iron. This will quickly lead to inaccuracy and frustration. Getting piecing wet will also give you puckers and wrinkles, which is sad. At the very least, oversteaming simply takes longer: to get rid of all that water you have to be at the ironing board longer, which slows you down.

My preference is to keep a spray bottle of water at my ironing surface and give my patchwork a little mist when I need it. I drop a touch of linen spray into the mix, which imparts a pleasant fragrance as I work.

PRESSING BASICS

- Press; don't iron. Bring the iron down gently and firmly on the fabric from above in a firm, stamping motion. Don't slide or smush a hot iron across the surface of patchwork.

- Press seams to one side.

- Whenever possible, press toward the darker fabric. This helps any seam not show through a light fabric used in the quilt top.

- Always press a seam before crossing it with another.

- Press the seams within the blocks of adjacent rows in opposite directions. This is so they will nest as the rows are sewn together.

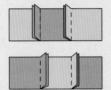

Press seams in opposite directions so they nest when joined.

WHOOPS!

Taking seams out of patchwork you've sewn incorrectly is inevitable, so put out of your mind the idea that if you have to rip out, you are a bad sewist. Sometimes you'll have turned your pieces without realizing it; sometimes you put your bobbin in backward and your stitch is all weird. It could be many things, and it will be.

My method for taking out a seam is to use my seam ripper to sever every third stitch or so on the back, or wrong side, of the patchwork. Once you do that, it's very easy to gently pull apart the seam. You won't be damaging the fabric, and you won't have as many loose fibers to manage afterward.

ASSEMBLING THE TOP

JOINING THE BLOCKS

Toward the end of every project in this book, as in most quilt patterns, you'll see the words, "Sew blocks into rows. Join rows to complete the top." This means that after all the blocks for a quilt are complete, arrange them on the floor or on a design wall. Pin and sew together the blocks in vertical or horizontal rows. (You can also join rows diagonally, but as there are no diagonal rows in this book, we'll skip that approach. Next book.)

As you did in individual blocks, press seams in opposite directions from row to row. After all the rows are constructed, join the rows, nesting the pressed seam allowances so the blocks align. To make the task of assembling these large quilt tops manageable, first join the rows into pairs and then join those pairs, rather than adding a single row to an increasingly large top. Some of the instructions in this book suggest working in quadrants; same principle.

Working with smaller chunks is easier than working with very long rows. You always want to sew the shortest distance possible because sewing an accurate seam is not always easy. Sometimes you can't avoid long rows. But when possible, shorten them to make life easier.

After the top is complete, do one more round of pressing. Press the wrong side first, carefully clipping and removing excess thread. Then press the right side, doing your best to get all the seams to lie flat.

ESSENTIAL TOOL: THE DESIGN WALL

A design wall is any wall or section of wall covered with felt, flannel, or a fabricated cover that allows you to "stick" pieces of patchwork up without adhesive. When you place blocks and other pieces on a design wall, you can step back and look at your work from a distance, move things around, and see how the whole quilt reads from the most beneficial perspective—level, about six feet back. (Refer to Design Fundamentals, page 18, for further explanation.)

If your design wall is just a piece of flannel or a store-bought hangable design wall, it can also transport a quilt in progress. Simply take it down with care and either roll or fold it up with all your pieces inside. They will stay mostly in place, but unfold or unroll it carefully.

BORDERS

Directions for adding borders are included with the instructions for each quilt, but here are some general notes for successful borders.

- Before you cut border pieces or add anything to the quilt, measure the completed *inner* quilt top. Measure through the center of the quilt rather than along the edges, as the edges may have stretched as you worked with it. Use this middle measurement to determine the exact length to mark and cut borders.

- Cut the borders the desired finished length plus ½″ for seam allowances.

- To make sure you're lining everything up correctly, fold the border strips in half and in half again. Press lightly just at the folds to create quarter marks on each border. Align these marks with the center and quarter points of the quilt; then pin the whole border to the quilt. Now that you know it's lined up nice, sew it on.

PUTTING TOGETHER THE LAYERS

LAYERING

A quilt is made of three layers: the pieced top, the batting, and the backing—this is called the quilt sandwich. When the three layers are put together and sewn together, usually with a pretty pattern, then it's a quilt. A popular adage goes, "It's not a quilt until it's quilted."

BATTING

The batting is the filler in the quilt sandwich. When purchasing a batt, read the details on the package and consider the intended use of the quilt. Is it for display? Heavy use? Are you submitting to a contest? Don't care one way or the other? Regardless, talk to experienced quilters about what they use.

Batting Choices
- 100% polyester: very durable and warm, no shrinkage
- 100% cotton: very flat, an old-fashioned look
- Poly blend: low-loft like cotton, but stable like poly
- Others: silk, flannel, wool, or something else; read up before you buy

BATT:
short for batting

Whatever you select, unroll the batt and let it lie open for a few hours to soften any folds. You can also stick the batt in the dryer on low for 5–10 minutes.

MAKING THE QUILT SANDWICH

If you are sending your quilt for longarm quilting, your quilter will prep the quilt for her machine. If you're doing your own machine quilting, use the following steps to prepare the sandwich.

1. Fold the backing in half lengthwise and press it to give yourself a centerline. Place the backing, wrong side up, on a large flat surface (the floor works). To keep the backing taught, secure it with masking tape at the corners and sides.

2. Fold the batting in half lengthwise and place it on top of the backing, aligning the fold with the center crease line of the backing. Open out the batting and smooth and pat down any wrinkly parts.

3. Fold the quilt top in half lengthwise, right sides together, and place it on top of the batting, aligning the fold with the center of the batting. Open out the top and remove any loose threads.

IMPORTANT

Make sure the backing and batt are at least 4″ larger than the top on all sides. If you're giving the quilt to a longarmer, make sure you give her anywhere from 4″ to 10″ extra on all sides. Check with your longarmer to determine what is needed.

BASTING

Using safety pins, baste the quilt by placing pins through all three layers of the sandwich, each about one fist-width away from the next.

BASTING:

to hold together the three layers of a quilt with long, loose stitches or with safety pins in preparation for sewing

I recommend using pins from the quilt shop designed specifically for pin basting. These pins are bent to help scoop up the layers. A grapefruit spoon is a good tool to use to close pin after pin, as fingers can get sore pin basting big quilts like these. There are also special tools made just for closing basting pins.

Quilter's basting pin

QUILTING

You can quilt three ways: by hand, by machine, or by check. Translation: You can hand quilt your quilt, quilt it on your machine, or pay a longarm quilter to do it for you.

The quilts in this book were machine quilted on a full-length longarm by a professional longarmer or by me on a mid-arm quilting machine.

I am the first to admit that I have little experience with hand quilting; it's not a skill anyone has clamored to teach me, and I have not clamored to ask. I may dive into hand quilting someday, but it doesn't bother me, and hopefully won't bother you, that hand quilting is seen as a luxury, even a novelty these days, like a handwritten letter. *There is no shame in machine quilting or in sending your quilt to a longarm quilter.* How your quilt gets quilted is often a question o*f how much* time you have, how much money you want to spend, and how your quilt will be used.

There are many excellent books dedicated to the skill and art of machine quilting (see Resources, page 127, for suggested reading), so let's just go over the basics to get you going.

Machine Quilting

Decide whether you want to do straight-line (or gently curving) quilting or free-motion quilting. Either way, consult your sewing machine manual as needed to switch to the proper foot and, for free-motion quilting, to lower the feed dogs.

For straight-line quilting, use a machine quilting or walking foot. If your machine has a dual feed, engage it. Many sewing machines come with an attachable bar that can help guide you in straight-line quilting.

For free-motion quilting, use a stippling, darning, free-motion, or machine-embroidery presser foot and lower the feed dogs on the machine so that you can freely manipulate the quilt. Choose a continuous-line pattern so you won't need to start and stop much. Use both hands so that you get nice, even stitches.

Consult your manual with questions regarding tension settings and by all means, take a class or have an experienced friend help you if you're quilting for the first time.

In each project, you'll find suggestions for quilting. You'll see how the quilt I made was quilted, but these are just single options out of countless possibilities.

LITTLE MITTENS

Quilting gloves are a beautiful thing. A thin coat of rubber on each finger of these lightweight gloves helps you grip and control the quilt as you move it through the machine. There are several brands available—choose the ones that feel comfortable to you.

FINISHING UP

BINDING

Without binding, the edges of a quilt would come apart. The standard method is a French fold binding, which is just a fancy way of saying double-fold binding. This kind of binding is easier to apply than single-fold, and the double thickness is more durable.

The amount of binding needed for each quilt in this book is included with the finishing instructions. Generally, you will need enough binding to go around the perimeter of the quilt plus 8″–10″ for mitering the corners and ending the binding. I cut strips for double-fold binding 2½″ wide, so 1 to 1½ yards of fabric will usually make enough binding to finish a big quilt.

Making and Putting On Binding

1. Refer to the individual project instructions for the amount of binding the quilt requires and the number of strips needed. As with other fabric strips, cut them across the fabric width.

2. Join the strips by placing them right sides together at right angles and sewing diagonal seams. Trim the excess to a ¼″ seam allowance.

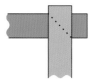

Join strips to make binding.

3. Here's where the French fold happens. Fold and press the long strip in half lengthwise, *wrong* sides together, giving you a double-layered binding. Watch your fingers as you do this. That iron is hot!

4. Make sure your machine is wearing its walking foot (or has the dual feed engaged). Starting at a point that's at least 12″ away from a corner, place the raw edges of the binding strip even with the raw edge of the quilt top.

5. Leave a tail at least 4″–6″ long and begin sewing with a ¼″ seam allowance, sewing through all 3 layers of the sandwich.

6. When you get to a corner, stop ¼″ away from it. Backstitch a few stitches and then remove the quilt from the machine.

7. Fold the binding up and away from the corner, forming a 45° angle.

Stop sewing ¼″ from corner; fold up binding.

8. Fold down the binding strip, creating a fold along the top edge of the quilt. Align the raw edges with the adjacent side of the quilt.

9. Begin stitching the next side at the top fold of the binding. Do all 4 corners this way. Continue sewing, and stop about 12″ from the beginning.

Fold down binding; continue stitching.

Finishing the Binding

1. Fold the ending tail of the binding back upon itself where it meets the beginning binding tail. From the fold, measure and mark the cut width of your binding strip. Cut the ending binding tail to this measurement. For example, if your binding is cut 2½″ wide, measure from the fold on the ending tail of the binding 2½″ and cut the binding tail to this length.

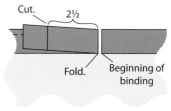

Cut.   2½

Fold.   Beginning of binding

Cut binding tail.

2. Open both tails. Place one tail on top of the other tail at right angles, right sides together. Mark a diagonal line from corner to corner and stitch on the line. Check you've done it correctly and that the binding fits the quilt; then trim the seam allowance to ¼″. Press open.

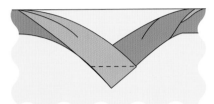

Stitch ends of binding diagonally.

3. Refold the binding and stitch this binding section in place on the quilt.

4. Using good (meaning sharp) shears, trim the edges of the quilt. You should trim the backing and batting about ⅛″ *beyond* the binding edge, just enough to fill the binding when you turn it to the back. This makes the binding look better, and it is more durable if it's filled rather than

hollow. Fold the binding over the raw edges to the quilt back and hand stitch.

5. Turn the binding to the back. You can sew down the binding by hand or on your sewing machine, using the walking foot. At the corners, finish the mitering by folding in the adjacent sides on the back of the quilt and placing several blind stitches in the miter, both front and back.

BLACK AND WHITE BINDING

I typically bind my quilts in black or white. There are exceptions. The black binding functions as a hard frame for the quilt, like a letterbox for a film or the border of a photograph. When black just won't do (as with *Whisper*, page 54), white is the obvious choice; consider that Polaroid pictures are framed this way. For the most part I stick to this rule, but you must bind your quilts in whatever fabric pleases you.

LABELS AND CHARMS

With a tragically small number of exceptions, the quilts we have from yesteryear (think late 1700s to 1950 or so) were not labeled, so we don't know who made them or when they were made. Women who had to make quilts rarely thought to label them. Back then, a quilt was a like a loaf of bread: maybe you baked a good one, but to autograph it seemed weird, even arrogant. In the case of a special occasion such as a wedding or when a

quiltmaker was particularly proud of a quilt, she might have put her name on it. We cherish that information today.

It's a shame we don't know the names of these brilliant designers, if for no other reason than to give them a reverential nod when we put one of their blocks in our latest quilt. Don't be like them. Throw family members, quilt collectors, and historians a bone by labeling your quilt.

OPTION 1: FABRIC LABEL

There are many ways to make quilt labels these days, but here's my go-to method:

1. Decide the size and shape of the label, draw the shape on the dull (paper) side of a piece of freezer paper, and cut it out.

2. Press the waxy side of the freezer paper to the wrong side of a piece of muslin or other light-colored fabric. This will stabilize the fabric and make writing easier.

3. With a fabric-marking pen, write any information you think is important, such as the following:

- "Made by" and your name (the most important)

- The place the quilt was made (second most important)

- When the quilt was made

- Any special occasion or reason why the quilt was made

- The name of the quilt (if you've named it)

4. Trim the fabric, allowing enough extra fabric to turn under for a clean edge.

5. Hand stitch the label to the back of the quilt. A good spot for a quilt label is the lower left- or right-hand corner, but, of course, you can put it anywhere.

OPTION 2: QUILT CHARM

In 2013, I decided I wanted another option for labeling quilts, so I created Quilt Charms. A Quilt Charm is a small medallion of 14-karat gold, rose gold, or sterling silver–plated brass that gives information about a quilt. It is designed to be personalized, just like a cloth label. You can have a Quilt Charm engraved with whatever letters, text, or numbers you want, and then stitch the charm onto a quilt. I like the lower right-hand corner, but I've also put charms on the front. Aside from being an arguably more durable way to label your quilt, Quilt Charms add an elegant finishing touch. They are washable, virtually weightless, and totally smooth. I stitch mine on with perle cotton, but embroidery floss or multiple rounds through the rings with durable poly thread will work, too. Personalized Quilt Charms can be ordered through my website, maryfons.com.

Quilt Charms. I engraved an extra message on each charm, something else to warm the recipient.

Cloth labels like this allow for lots of information; be sure to use a permanent fabric marking pen when writing. Affix to quilt by hand stitching; you could also use a strong fusible.

PROJECTS

NORTHBOUND

MADE BY MARY FONS, QUILTED BY SALLY EVANSHANK

Finished quilt: 108″ × 126″   Finished block: 9″ × 9″

In *Northbound*, flocks of Flying Geese soar east, west, and north, of course. Deep indigo and tree bark tones are set against a starry night. A bit of red here and there, a touch of cream, and you've got a quilt fit for serious hibernation.

As you piece this one, play around with the placement of the blues, reds, and browns. Eliminate the lighter blues if you like; make the red fabric gold if you want. This version was quilted with birds to carry the migrating geese thing, but I have to say: I slightly regret not going with bears.

MATERIALS

BLOCKS

- ⅞ yard total scrappy reds
- 3½ yards total scrappy navies and blues
- 2 yards total scrappy browns and greiges (a color between beige and gray)
- ⅞ yard total creams and rogue prints (see Rogue Blocks, page 23)
- ⅞ yard total dove gray prints
- 4 yards total subtly printed black for blocks

PIECED BORDER

- 3⅛ yards dotted black
- 1¾ yards solid black

BACKING

- 11¼ yards total scraps or yardage

BINDING

- 1 yard solid black

BATTING

- 116″ × 134″

SPECIAL TOOLS (OPTIONAL)

- Fons & Porter Half and Quarter Ruler

CUTTING

If you need help with cutting, take a look at Cutting (page 25).

SCRAPPY REDS

- *If using optional ruler,** cut 4 strips 3½″ × width of fabric; subcut into 33 quarter-square triangles to make 11 blocks. *Otherwise,* cut 2 strips 7¼″ × width of fabric; subcut into 9 squares 7¼″ × 7¼″ and cut each square in half diagonally twice to yield 36 quarter-square triangles (there will be 3 left over).
- Cut 6 strips 2″ × width of fabric for sides of blocks.

SCRAPPY NAVIES AND BLUES

- *If using optional ruler,** cut 17 strips 3½″ × width of fabric; subcut into 162 quarter-square triangles to make 54 blocks. *Otherwise,* cut 9 strips 7¼″ × width of fabric; subcut into 41 squares 7¼″ × 7¼″ and cut each square in half diagonally twice to yield 164 quarter-square triangles (there will be 2 left over).
- Cut 27 strips 2″ × width of fabric for sides of blocks.

SCRAPPY BROWNS AND GREIGES

- *If using optional ruler,** cut 10 strips 3½″ × width of fabric; subcut into 96 quarter-square triangles to make 32 blocks. *Otherwise,* cut 5 strips 7¼″ × width of fabric; subcut into 24 squares 7¼″ × 7¼″ and cut each square in half diagonally twice to yield 96 quarter-square triangles.
- Cut 16 strips 2″ × width of fabric for sides of blocks.

CREAMS AND ROGUE PRINTS

- *If using optional ruler,** cut 4 strips 3½″ × width of fabric; subcut into 36 quarter-square triangles to make 12 blocks. *Otherwise,* cut 2 strips 7¼″ × width of fabric; subcut into 9 squares 7¼″ × 7¼″ and cut each square in half diagonally twice to yield 36 quarter-square triangles.
- Cut 6 strips 2″ × width of fabric for sides of blocks.

NOTE

This is the biggest quilt in the book. It's all downhill from here.

DOVE GRAY PRINTS

- *If using optional ruler,** cut 4 strips 3½" × width of fabric; subcut into 33 quarter-square triangles to make 11 blocks.

  Otherwise, cut 2 strips 7¼" × width of fabric; subcut into 9 squares 7¼" × 7¼" and cut each square in half diagonally twice to yield 36 quarter-square triangles (there will be 3 left over).

- Cut 6 strips 2" × width of fabric for sides of blocks.

SUBTLY PRINTED BLACK

- *If using optional ruler,** cut 36 strips 3½" × width of fabric; subcut into 720 half-square triangles to be used as background for 120 blocks.

  Otherwise, cut 36 strips 3⅞" × width of fabric; subcut into 360 squares 3⅞" × 3⅞" and cut each square in half diagonally to yield 720 half-square triangles.

DOTTED BLACK

- *If using optional ruler,** cut 15 strips 3½" × width of fabric; subcut into 144 quarter-square triangles to make 48 border blocks.

  Otherwise, cut 8 strips 7¼" × width of fabric; subcut into 36 squares 7¼" × 7¼" and cut each square in half diagonally twice to yield 144 quarter-square triangles.

- Cut 24 strips 2" × width of fabric for sides of border blocks.

SOLID BLACK

- *If using optional ruler,** cut 15 strips 3½" × width of fabric; subcut into 288 half-square triangles to make 48 border blocks.

  Otherwise, cut 15 strips 3⅞" × width of fabric; subcut into 144 squares 3⅞" × 3⅞" and cut each square in half diagonally to yield 288 half-square triangles.

- Cut 13 strips 2½" × width of fabric for binding.

* *Fons & Porter Half and Quarter Ruler*

First—if you are in love—that's a good thing—
that's about the best thing that can happen to anyone.
Don't let anyone make it small or light to you.

JOHN STEINBECK

CONSTRUCTION

If you need help with construction, take a look at Construction Basics (page 24). Seam allowances are ¼".

FLYING GEESE BLOCKS

1. Create a Flying Geese unit (G-unit) by sewing 1 subtly printed black half-square triangle to each side of a color print quarter-square triangle. Make 2 more of these G-units for 1 block.

Flying Geese unit

2. Sew together 3 G-units, making sure all 3 face the same direction.

Sew together Flying Geese.

3. Sew 2"-wide strips to both sides of the block. Trim the strips to complete 1 block.

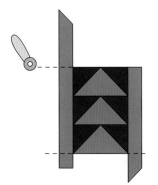

Add side borders to block and trim.

TIPS

- You could cut the 2"-wide strips so they each measure 9½" in length, but I didn't do that. I kept the strips long, sewed them onto the sides of my blocks, and then trimmed. This seemed to be faster.

- Use a large basket or bowl for the strips. Toss them in and mix them up like spaghetti; this helps randomize what you pull out.

4. Repeat to make a total of 120 blocks.

PIECED BORDER BLOCKS

1. Create blocks in the same manner as above using black and dotted black. Make a total of 48 border blocks.

2. Sew together 12 border blocks for the left side border. Sew together 11 blocks each for the top and bottom borders. Sew together 14 blocks for the right side border.

Border assembly

QUILT ASSEMBLY

Take a look at the quilt photo (page 40) and the quilt assembly diagram (below).

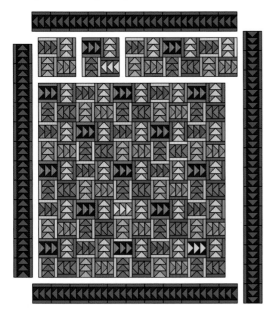

1. Sew together the blocks, alternating north-pointing Geese and east- and west-pointing Geese.

2. Assemble the blocks in quadrants to reduce the number of long rows you need to sew together.

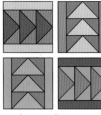 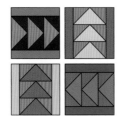

Work in quadrants.

TIP

The arrows in *Northbound* never point south, always north, east, or west, except in the border. This helps as you arrange blocks on your design wall as well as when you start joining rows: if you find a block pointing down, you've got something turned the wrong way.

3. Sew together the quadrants to create rows. Press the seams in alternate directions so they nest when the rows are sewn together. Sew together the rows.

4. Sew the left border to the quilt top, then add the top and bottom borders, and then add the right side border. (Take a look at Borders, page 33, as needed.)

FINISHING

If you need help with finishing, take a look at Putting Together the Layers (page 33) and Finishing Up (page 35).

1. Sew together yardage or scraps as needed to make the backing 4″–10″ bigger on all sides than the quilt top.

2. Layer the backing, batting, and quilt top. Baste and quilt as you please.

3. Create French fold binding in black fabric. Sew the binding to the quilt.

4. Crawl under for a long, deep sleep.

B-SIDE

When Mom and I were lecturing in Shipshewana, Indiana, I showed a picture of this quilt in progress. I told the audience how the Geese always face north, and my mother suggested I put an arrow on the back, a kind of "This Side Up" sign. I thought it was a great idea, so I promised her and the crowd I'd do just that.

Quilt Charm

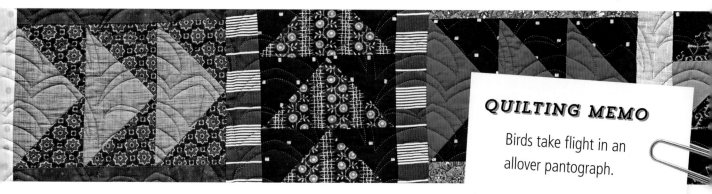

QUILTING MEMO

Birds take flight in an allover pantograph.

FOREST PRESERVE

MADE BY MARY FONS

Finished quilt: 84″ × 102″   Finished unit: 3″ × 3″

There's something about a forest that stirs even the most wizened of hearts. Blame Shakespeare—so much of his romantic action plays out amongst the trees.

Forest Preserve is made up entirely of half-square triangles. I have made several versions of this quilt over the years; I'm soothed by the undulating, wavelike effect. The solid navy triangles slow down the color opposite them—in this case, more than 25 different greens. I have made this quilt using navy and pink, and also with navy and white. Works every time.

MATERIALS

BLOCKS

- 5½ yards total medium green and light green (Each of the 25 different greens I used totaled about ¼ yard.)

- 5½ yards solid dark navy blue

BACKING

- 7¾ yards total scraps or yardage

BINDING

- ⅞ yard solid black

BATTING

- 92″ × 110″

TIP

The trick to this quilt is to keep the two halves of the half-square triangles in high contrast. Don't go too dark with your greens; otherwise the half-square triangle units will read as squares. If you're not sure about the values, put the fabric up on your design wall, step back 6–10 feet, and check it out.

CUTTING

If you need help with cutting, take a look at Cutting (page 25).

GREENS

- *If using optional ruler,* cut 48 strips** 3½″ × width of fabric; subcut into as many half-square triangles as you can. You will need 952 half-square triangles.*
  Otherwise, cut 48 strips** 3⅞″ × width of fabric; subcut into 476 squares 3⅞″ × 3⅞″ and cut each square in half diagonally to yield 952 half-square triangles.

NAVY BLUE

- *If using optional ruler,* cut 48 strips** 3½″ × width of fabric; subcut into 952 half-square triangles.*
  Otherwise, cut 48 strips** 3⅞″ × width of fabric; subcut into 476 squares 3⅞″ × 3⅞″ and cut each square in half diagonally to yield 952 half-square triangles.

BINDING

- Cut 11 strips 2½″ × width of fabric.

* Fons & Porter Half and Quarter Ruler

** Because you'll be pulling from your scraps, cut as many strips as needed to get the required number of half-square triangles.

> The time you enjoy wasting is not wasted time.
> BERTRAND RUSSELL

CONSTRUCTION

If you need help with construction, take a look at Construction Basics (page 24). Seam allowances are ¼".

HALF-SQUARE TRIANGLE BLOCKS

Create a half-square triangle block by joining a green triangle to a navy blue triangle. You will make 952 of these. (There, there. You'll be okay. It's worth it. Trust me.)

Make half-square triangle blocks.

QUILT ASSEMBLY

Take a look at the quilt photo (page 48) and the quilt assembly diagram (below).

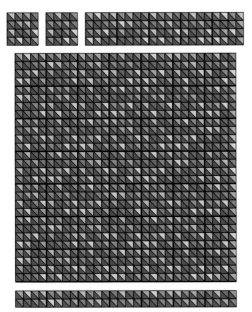

NOTE: As you put together all the blocks into rows and quadrants, press the seams in alternate directions so they nest when the rows and quadrants are sewn together.

1. Work in quadrants to assemble the blocks. Sew together 4 half-square triangle blocks into a row. Create 3 more of these rows. Sew together these 4 rows to create 1 quadrant. Repeat to make a total of 56 quadrants.

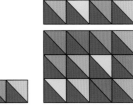

Make quadrants.

2. Sew together the quadrants into rows.

3. Sew together the remaining half-square triangle blocks into 4-block rows. Sew 2 rows together to create a rectangle block. Sew these 7 rectangles together to create the last row.

Make rectangles.

4. Sew together the rows to complete the top.

FINISHING

If you need help with finishing, take a look at Putting Together the Layers (page 33) and Finishing Up (page 35).

1. Sew together yardage or scraps as needed to make the backing 4″–10″ bigger on all sides than the quilt top.

2. Layer the backing, batting, and quilt top. Baste and quilt as you please.

3. Create French fold binding in black fabric. Sew the binding to the quilt.

B-SIDE

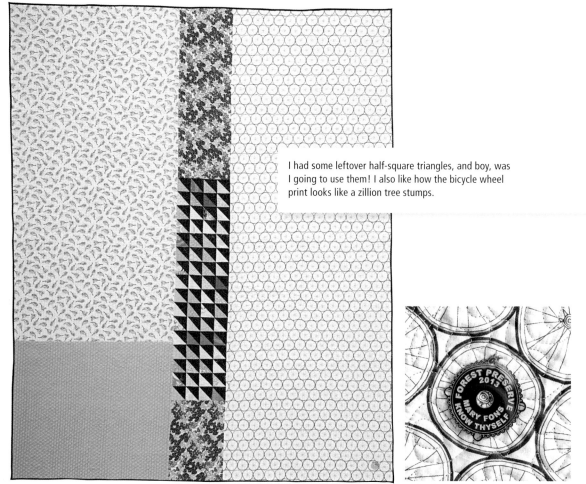

I had some leftover half-square triangles, and boy, was I going to use them! I also like how the bicycle wheel print looks like a zillion tree stumps.

Quilt Charm

QUILTING MEMO

Freehand stippling was lots of fun here, and I like how the curves contrast with the geometric half-square triangles.

WHISPER

MADE BY MARY FONS, QUILTED BY SALLY EVANSHANK

Finished quilt: 90″ × 104″   Finished triangle unit: 4⅝″ at base, 4″ tall

Here's what I love: snowdrifts, vanilla frosting, crisp hotel linen, petticoats, Lamb Chop, tissues, the tile in my bathroom. What do these things have in common? They are all shades of white.

This quilt is made with shirting prints and white fabrics and is truly a dream-come-true quilt for a lover of ecru, bone, and paper whites. As soon as it was in process, I was as happy as a clam (another great shade of white, incidentally).

The pattern is a classic Thousand Pyramid, hundreds of equilateral triangles. I used a special ruler to cut my pieces from strips, which I recommend; a die cutter would be great for this quilt, too. If you have neither, making an old-fashioned template using the pattern (page 58) will do the trick.

MATERIALS

TRIANGLES

- 5 yards total assorted off-whites (shirtings, ditzy prints, small dots, and so on)

- 5 yards total assorted snow or bright whites

BACKING

- 8½ yards total scraps or yardage

BINDING

- ⅞ yard white or off-white

BATTING

- 98″ × 112″

SPECIAL TOOLS (OPTIONAL)

- Fons & Porter Pyramid Ruler

CUTTING

If you need help with cutting, take a look at Cutting (page 25). Cut the triangles using either the Fons & Porter Pyramid Ruler or a template made using the pattern (page 58).

OFF-WHITES

- Cut 38 strips 4½″ wide; subcut into 520 triangles.

SNOW OR BRIGHT WHITES

- Cut 38 strips 4½″ wide; subcut into 520 triangles.

Cut triangles.

BINDING

- Cut 11 strips 2½″ × width of fabric.

MAKE YOUR OWN PYRAMID TEMPLATE

Before the quilt world exploded with special rulers for every shape, die-cutting systems, and so on, the template was much more a part of a quilter's experience.

With a few simple items from around the house or a quick trip to the quilt shop, you can easily make a template. Note that you'll be using your template to *draw* around, not *cut* around with your rotary cutter. Your homemade template will be far too thin to withstand being sliced around with the rotary cutter.

You need something sturdy from which to cut the template, so pick paper heavier than cardstock but thin enough to cut accurately. Template plastic is obviously a great choice, but I remember my mother making templates from cereal boxes.

Draw the template shape on the plastic or cardboard with a fine-point indelible marker. It's important that your marker be thin because a thick line will create confusion: do you cut out your piece on the inside or the outside of the thick line? A fine line solves this.

Using a craft knife or scissors suited for the job (*not* your fabric scissors), cut out the template. Place it on the right side of the fabric, trace around it onto the fabric, and cut out the fabric on the drawn line.

CONSTRUCTION

1. Sew an off-white triangle to a snow-white triangle. Take care to align the triangles precisely.

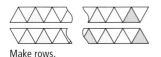

Sew together triangles, inverting every other piece.

2. Repeat to sew together 40 triangles, alternating off-white and snow white. All the off-whites will be pointing up; all the bright or snow whites will be inverted or pointing down. Press all the seams to one side in row A and to the other side in row B. Note that row A starts with a triangle pointing up, while row B starts with a triangle inverted. Make 13 of each row.

Make rows.

QUILT ASSEMBLY

Take a look at the quilt photo (page 54) and the quilt assembly diagram (below).

Sew the rows together in pairs; then trim the ends ¼" beyond the end point. Sew these sets together to complete the top.

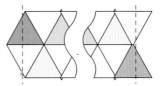

Trim ends 1/4″ beyond end points.

FINISHING

If you need help with finishing, take a look at Putting Together the Layers (page 33) and Finishing Up (page 35).

1. Sew together yardage or scraps as needed to make the backing 4″–10″ bigger on all sides than the quilt top.

2. Layer the backing, batting, and quilt top. Baste and quilt as you please.

3. Create French fold binding in black fabric. Sew the binding to the quilt.

4. Whisper a really good secret.

> The only difference between a caprice and a life-long passion is that the caprice lasts a little longer.
>
> OSCAR WILDE, *THE PICTURE OF DORIAN GRAY*

B-SIDE

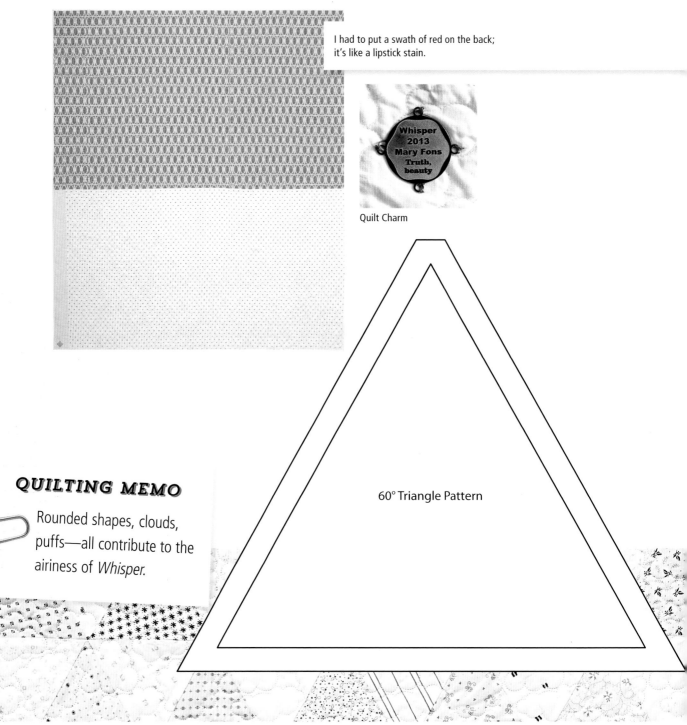

I had to put a swath of red on the back;
it's like a lipstick stain.

Whisper
2013
Mary Fons
Truth,
beauty

Quilt Charm

60° Triangle Pattern

QUILTING MEMO

Rounded shapes, clouds,
puffs—all contribute to the
airiness of *Whisper*.

THE ROYAL WE

MADE BY MARY FONS, QUILTED BY EBONY LOVE

Finished quilt: 80″ × 104″   Finished block: 12″ × 12″

The inspiration for this quilt came in New York City. I was walking down East 19th Street and was stopped in my tracks by a quilt in the window of an antiques shop. Solid black and white blocks topped rich green, gold, and red. I thought the quilt looked masculine and weighty, like it could take on New York City and win.

As you select fabric for this one, take care with the reds and greens and gold. To avoid garishness, these fabrics should be very close to one another in both contrast and value. Note, too, they're all a little muted; there's gold in the green, there's a touch of green in a few of the reds, and the gold is never yellow. Give yourself plenty of time and options when auditioning fabrics here.

MATERIALS

BLOCKS AND BORDERS

- 1⅛ yards total yellow-greens and emerald greens
- ⅜ yard total golds
- 1⅜ yards total rusty reds, brick reds, and so on
- 3 yards solid black
- 2¼ yards solid white

SOLID BORDERS

- ¾ yard green
- ¾ yard gold
- ¾ yard red

> **TIP**
>
> I don't use batiks very often, but this quilt benefited from the watery look of several green- and gold-colored batiks.

BACKING

- 7½ yards total scraps or yardage

BINDING

- ⅞ yard solid black

BATTING

- 88″ × 112″

SPECIAL TOOLS (OPTIONAL)

- Fons & Porter Quarter Inch Seam Marker
- Fons & Porter Half and Quarter Ruler

CUTTING

If you need help with cutting, take a look at Cutting (page 25).

GREENS

- Cut 8 strips 4½″ × width of fabric; subcut into 72 squares 4½″ × 4½″ for Nine-Patch blocks.
- Cut 8 strips 2½″ × width of fabric from 1 green for border.

GOLDS

- Cut 2 strips 4½″ × width of fabric; subcut into 18 squares 4½″ × 4½″ for Nine-Patch blocks.
- Cut 8 strips 2½″ × width of fabric from 1 gold for border.

REDS

- Cut 10 strips 4½″ × width of fabric; subcut into 89 red squares 4½″ × 4½″ for Nine-Patch and Star blocks.
- Cut 9 strips 2½″ × width of fabric from 1 red for border.

SOLID BLACK

- Cut 5 strips 5¼″ × width of fabric; subcut into 34 squares 5¼″ × 5¼″ for hourglass units.
- Cut 5 strips 4⅞″ × width of fabric; subcut into 34 squares 4⅞″ × 4⅞″ for half-square triangle units.
- Cut 9 strips 2½″ × width of fabric for inner border.

For outer border:

- *If using optional ruler,* * cut 7 strips 2½″ × width of fabric; subcut into 94 quarter-square triangles.
  Otherwise, cut 3 strips 5¼″ × width of fabric; subcut into 24 squares 5¼″ × 5¼″ and cut each square in half diagonally twice to yield 94 quarter-square triangles.

SOLID WHITE

- Cut 5 strips 5¼″ × width of fabric; subcut into 34 squares 5¼″ × 5¼″ for hourglass units.

- Cut 5 strips 4⅞″ × width of fabric; subcut into 34 squares 4⅞″ × 4⅞″ for half-square triangle units.

> The evolution of the human race will not be accomplished in the ten thousand years of tame animals, but in the million years of wild animals, because man is and always will be a wild animal.
>
> CHARLES DARWIN

For outer border:

- *If using optional ruler,** cut 6 strips 2½″ × width of fabric; subcut into 90 quarter-square triangles.
  Otherwise, cut 3 strips 5¼″ × width of fabric; subcut into 23 squares 5¼″ × 5¼″ and cut each square in half diagonally twice to yield 90 quarter-square triangles.

BINDING

- Cut 10 strips 2½″ × width of fabric.

* Fons & Porter Half and Quarter Ruler

CONSTRUCTION

NINE-PATCH BLOCKS

Arrange the 4½″ squares for the Nine-Patch blocks. Sew the squares in rows. Press the seams in alternate directions so they nest when the rows are sewn together. Sew together the rows to make the Nine-Patch block.

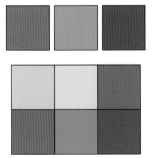

Nine-Patch blocks; make 18.

HALF-SQUARE TRIANGLE UNITS

1. Place a 4⅞″ white square right sides together with a 4⅞″ black square. Place the Fons & Porter Quarter Inch Seam Marker across the back of the white square from corner to corner and draw a line on either side of the ruler to mark the sewing lines. *Or* draw a line diagonally from corner to corner and then draw lines ¼″ away on both sides of the diagonal line to mark the sewing lines.

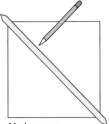

Mark squares.

2. Sew on the drawn lines; then press. Cut from corner to corner using a rotary cutter, creating 2 half-square triangle units.

Sew on lines.

3. Press the units open, toward the black fabric. Trim, if needed, to 4½″ × 4½″, keeping the seams exactly in the corners. Make 68 half-square triangle units.

HOURGLASS UNITS

1. Place a 5¼″ white square right sides together with a 5¼″ black square. Mark, sew, and cut just like you did the half-square triangle units above.

2. Press the unit open, toward the black fabric. Put the pair of triangle squares together, taking care to place opposite fabrics/colors facing. Mark the new seam from corner to corner, perpendicular to the first seam.

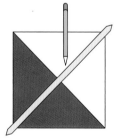
Mark second seam.

3. Stitch along both drawn lines, as before. Press; then cut them apart.

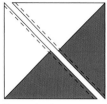
Sew and cut.

4. Open and press to reveal the hourglass unit. You'll need 68 of these.

Hourglass unit; make 68.

STAR BLOCKS

Arrange the pieces for the Star block as shown. Sew the units into rows. Press the seams in alternate directions so they nest when the rows are sewn together. Sew together the rows to make the Star block. You will make 17 of these blocks.

Star block; make 17.

BORDERS

Take a look at Borders (page 33) as needed.

For the solid-color borders, sew individual strips together end to end, so that you have long strips.

For the pieced outer border:

1. Place a white quarter-square triangle on a black quarter-square triangle, offsetting the points, and sew together.

Offset triangle points

2. For each of the side borders, sew 25 white and 26 black quarter-square triangles together; for the top and bottom borders, sew 20 white and 21 black quarter-square triangles each.

Make border.

QUILT ASSEMBLY

Take a look at the quilt photo (page 60) and the quilt assembly diagram (below).

1. Sew together the blocks into rows. Press the seams in alternate directions so they nest when the rows are sewn together. Sew together the rows.

2. Measure the length of the quilt top and cut 2 green borders this length. Sew on the green side borders and press the seams toward the border. Then measure across the quilt and cut 2 green borders this length. Sew the borders to the top and bottom and press the seams toward the border. Repeat this process for each successive border, adding the sides and then the top and bottom borders, and ending with the black-and-white pieced border.

FINISHING

If you need help with finishing, take a look at Putting Together the Layers (page 33) and Finishing Up (page 35).

1. Sew together yardage or scraps as needed to make the backing 4″–10″ bigger on all sides than the quilt top.

2. Layer the backing, batting, and quilt top. Baste and quilt as you please.

3. Create French fold binding in black fabric. Sew the binding to the quilt.

4. Take Manhattan.

B-SIDE

More rich reds. Like roses!

The Royal
We
2013
Mary Fons

Make love,
not war

Quilt Charm

QUILTING MEMO

Heavy freehand lines lend a sophisticated air to this quilt without getting stuffy. Jeeves, more champagne, please.

FORMAL AFFAIR

MADE BY MARY FONS, QUILTED BY LUANN DOWNS

Finished quilt: 80″ × 98″   Finished block: 6″ × 6″

One of the best things about going to a fancy party is coming home, taking off your shoes and your makeup, and getting into bed. If there's a quilt on that bed, chances are good you've come home a touch earlier than most. When bed is heaven, why be anywhere else?

Formal Affair simply repeats a charming block that could be categorized as a Bow Tie.

I selected numerous champagne and gold tones for the ties but kept both the center and background of the block consistent throughout. A narrow double border adds bit of polish.

The color scheme also brings to mind a taxi-cab, which is a great way to arrive at or leave any party.

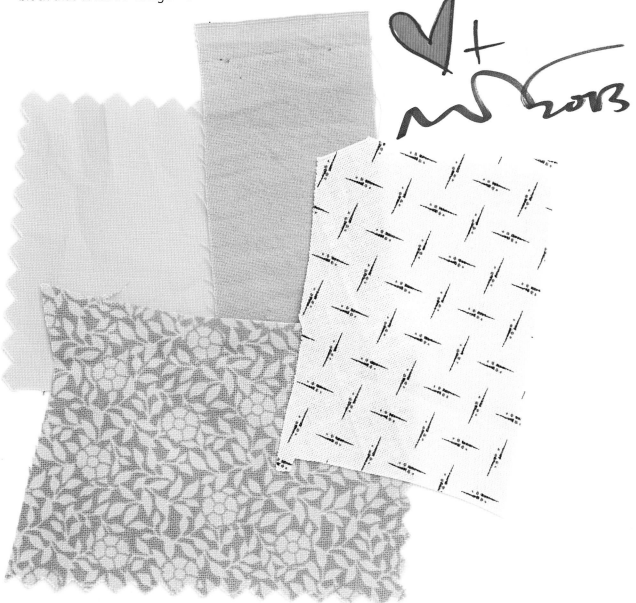

MATERIALS

BLOCKS AND BORDERS

- 4¼ yards solid charcoal gray for block background, plus ¾ yard for border

- 2¼ yards shirting print for middle of bow tie, plus ¾ yard for border

- 15 fat quarters of various medium to light yellows

BACKING

- 7½ yards total scraps or yardage

BINDING

- ⅞ yard solid black

BATTING

- 88″ × 106″

CUTTING

If you need help with cutting, take a look at Cutting (page 25).

CHARCOAL SOLID

- Cut 60 strips 2½″ × width of fabric; subcut into 360 rectangles 2½″ × 6½″.

- Cut 17 strips 1½″ × width of fabric for inner and outer borders.

SHIRTING PRINT

- Cut 30 strips 2½″ × width of fabric; subcut into 180 rectangles 2½″ × 6½″ for middle portion of bow tie.

- Cut 9 strips 2½″ × width of fabric for middle border.

YELLOW FAT QUARTERS

- From each fat quarter, cut 7 strips 2½″ × width of fabric; subcut into 48 squares 2½″ × 2½″, for a total of 720 squares.

BINDING

- Cut 10 strips 2½″ × width of fabric.

> In their first passions, women are in love with their lover; in the rest, with love.
> LA ROCHEFOUCAULD

CONSTRUCTION

If you need help with construction, take a look at Construction Basics (page 24). Seam allowances are ¼″.

1. Make the blocks using what's commonly known as "flippy corner" method: Place a yellow square facedown on the left side of a charcoal rectangle. Sew a diagonal seam from the upper left-

Sew diagonal seams.

hand corner to the lower right-hand corner. If you like, you can draw a sewing line from corner to corner before you stitch. Place a yellow square of a different shade facedown on the right side of the same rectangle. This time sew from the upper right-hand corner to the lower left-hand corner. Make 360.

2. Trim the excess to a ¼″ seam allowance and press open to reveal the triangle corner. This is Unit A.

Unit A; trim seam allowances to ¼″.   Press open.

3. Sew a Unit A to each side of a shirting rectangle to complete a block. Make 180 blocks, taking care to use 4 different yellow squares in each block.

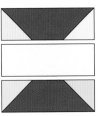

Make 180.

QUILT ASSEMBLY

Take a look at the quilt photo (page 68) and the quilt assembly diagram (below).

1. Sew together the blocks into rows. Press the seams in alternate directions so they nest when the rows are sewn together. Sew together the rows.

2. Sew the 1½″ charcoal strips end to end; then cut to length for borders. Measure the length of the quilt top and cut 2 side borders this length. Sew these borders on and press the seams toward the border. Measure the new width and cut the top and bottom borders to this length. Add them to the quilt top.

3. Sew the 2½″ shirting print strips end to end. Then measure and add the borders in the same manner as in Step 2.

4. Repeat this process for the final charcoal border.

FINISHING

If you need help with finishing, take a look at Putting Together the Layers (page 33) and Finishing Up (page 35).

1. Sew together yardage or scraps as needed to make the backing 4″–10″ bigger on all sides than the quilt top.

2. Layer the backing, batting, and quilt top. Baste and quilt as you please.

3. Create French fold binding in black fabric. Sew the binding to the quilt.

4. Envision your dream evening gown.

B-SIDE

The back of this quilt is fairly straightforward. You have to be careful with yellow; I didn't want anything competing with it, so I kept things quiet back here.

Quilt Charm

QUILTING MEMO

Corsages! Flowers seemed appropriate for a quilt on a date.

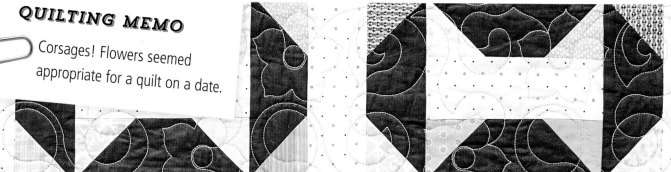

HELLO, THERE

MADE BY MARY FONS, QUILTED BY LUANN DOWNS

Finished quilt: 87½″ × 107½″   Finished block: 12½″ × 12½″

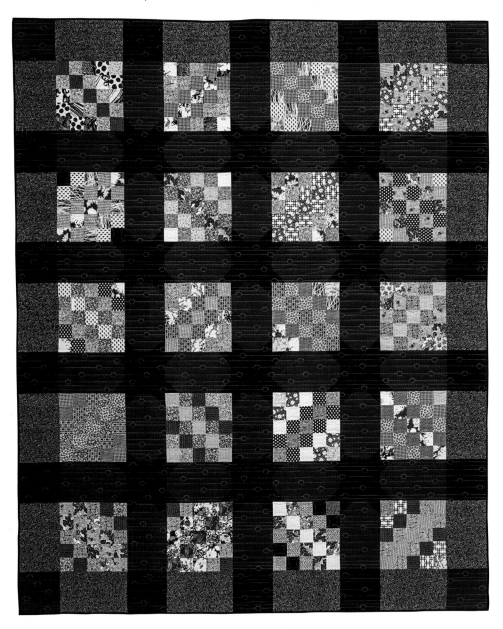

This quilt was inspired by an antique I saw at a show years ago. I snapped a blurry picture of a corner of it with my phone and found the picture a year later. I set about making my own version.

There are two layers to *Hello, There*. Which layer is the foreground and which is the background is tough to say, but the two work together. The patterned neutrals (page 16) go wild in the 25-Patch blocks but are reined in by the massive, bed-poster-like columns in solid bordeaux and navy.

This quilt is one of the quilts my mother understands the least, by the way, but I adore it.

MATERIALS

BLOCKS
- 3½ yards total assorted patterned neutrals (page 16)

BORDER, COLUMNS, AND SQUARES
- 3 yards bordeaux solid
- 1⅞ yards navy solid
- 1⅝ yards patterned gray for border

BACKING
- 8 yards total scraps or yardage

BINDING
- ¾ yard solid black

BATTING
- 96″ × 116″

SPECIAL TOOLS (OPTIONAL)
- Fons & Porter Half and Quarter Ruler

CUTTING

If you need help with cutting, take a look at Cutting (page 25).

PATTERNED NEUTRALS
- Cut 39 strips 3″ × width of fabric; subcut into 500 squares 3″ × 3″.

BORDEAUX
- *If using optional ruler,** cut 5 strips 3″ × width of fabric; subcut into 96 half-square triangles.
  Otherwise, cut 4 strips 3⅜″ × width of fabric; subcut into 48 squares 3⅜″ × 3⅜″ and cut each square in half diagonally to yield 96 half-square triangles.
- Cut 8 strips 8″ × width of fabric; subcut into 14 rectangles 8″ × 10½″ and 21 squares 8″ × 8″.
- Cut 4 strips 3″ × width of fabric; subcut into 48 squares 3″ × 3″.

NAVY
- *If using optional ruler,** cut 5 strips 3″ × width of fabric; subcut into 96 half-square triangles.
  Otherwise, cut 4 strips 3⅜″ × width of fabric; subcut into 48 squares 3⅜″ × 3⅜″ and cut each square in half diagonally to yield 96 half-square triangles.
- Cut 6 strips 8″ × width of fabric; subcut into 26 squares 8″ × 8″.

GRAY
- Cut 6 strips 8″ × width of fabric; subcut into 18 rectangles 8″ × 12½″ for border.

BINDING
- Cut 10 strips 2½″ × width of fabric.

* Fons & Porter Half and Quarter Ruler

O Love, set a word in my mouth for our meeting.

WILLIAM MORRIS

CONSTRUCTION

If you need help with construction, take a look at Construction Basics (page 24). Seam allowances are ¼".

25-PATCH BLOCKS

1. Select 25 varied 3″ squares. Arrange the patches on a table or design wall to ensure that the pieces are correctly placed. Note that the 5 fabrics that run down the diagonal center of each block form a noticeable diagonal. Take a look at the quilt photo (page 74) to see how the lines formed by these centerlines zigzag in opposite directions from one vertical row to the next.

Diagonal 25-patch block; make 20.

2. Sew the squares together, working in rows. Press the seams in opposite directions as you go so the seams nest when the rows are sewn together. Make 20 blocks.

SASHING

1. Create a half-square triangle unit by sewing together a navy triangle and a bordeaux triangle. Make 96 of these units.

Half-square triangle units; make 96.

2. Add 2 half-square triangle units from Step 1 to opposite sides of a 3″ bordeaux square, making sure the navy triangles face opposite directions, to form a Unit A. Make 48 Unit A's.

Unit A; make 48.

3. Add Unit A's to opposite sides of each 8″ bordeaux square to form the inner sashing units. Make 17 inner sashing units.

Inner sashing unit; make 17.

4. Add a Unit A to an end of each 8″ × 10½″ bordeaux rectangle to form the outer sashing units. Make 14 of these outer sashing units.

Outer sashing unit; make 14.

BORDER

Take a look at Borders (page 33) as needed.

1. For each side border, sew together 5 gray 8″ × 12½″ rectangles with 4 navy 8″ squares.

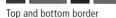

Side border

2. For the top border, join 4 gray 8″ × 12½″ rectangles with 3 navy 8″ squares. Add an 8″ bordeaux square to each end. Repeat for the bottom border.

Top and bottom border

QUILT ASSEMBLY

Take a look at the quilt photo (page 74) and the quilt assembly diagram (below).

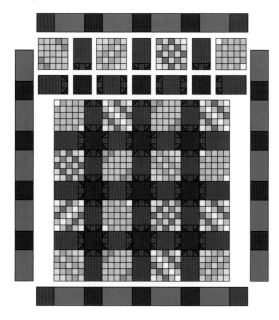

1. Sew together the blocks and sashing into rows.

2. Add the side borders and then the top and bottom borders.

FINISHING

If you need help with finishing, take a look at Putting Together the Layers (page 33) and Finishing Up (page 35).

1. Sew together yardage or scraps as needed to make the backing 4″–10″ bigger on all sides than the quilt top.

2. Layer the backing, batting, and quilt top. Baste and quilt as you please.

3. Create French fold binding in black fabric. Sew the binding to the quilt.

4. Greet your love with a smile.

B-SIDE

A bonus block is a nice touch. Guys like this quilt.

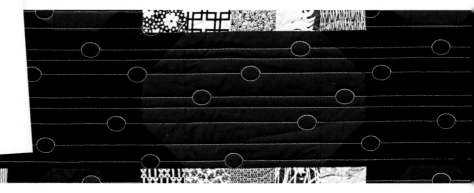

Hello, There
2013
Mary Fons
Desire begets
love

Quilt Charm

QUILTING MEMO

A little modern, a little abstract, but simple in order to not create noise within the crazy 25-Patches.

RUM RAISIN

MADE BY MARY FONS, QUILTED BY SALLY EVANSHANK

Finished quilt: 90″ × 100″   Finished block: 10″ × 10″

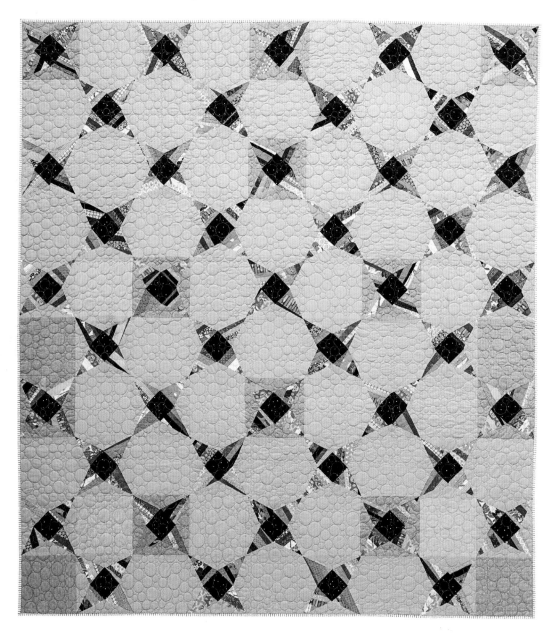

This quilt is a classic Rocky Road to Kansas pattern. Whenever I see a Rocky Road quilt, naturally I think of ice cream, but I prefer Rum Raisin.

It can be lonely, loving Rum Raisin. It's not a crowd pleaser like cookie dough or vanilla. But the unusual ice cream has an intriguing, sophisticated personality (kind of like pistachio, but with booze).

In homage to all my Rum Raisiennes, this quilt uses up loner scraps. I curated them only as far as deciding that the string-pieced portions would be in warm reds and oranges. I added a few pale shades to let it all breathe and black starry centers to tack it down. The Wedgwood blue behind the stars lets the orphan scraps shine.

MATERIALS

BLOCKS

- Scraps: approximately 4½ yards total dark reds, dark oranges, and medium oranges; a small amount of pale yellow and/or pale orange; plus a few black scraps tossed in for good measure

- 9⅝ yards Wedgwood blue solid (or variety of solid blues)

- 1⅛ yards dotted black

BACKING

- 8½ yards total scraps or yardage

BINDING

- ⅞ yard of white/black print

BATTING

- 98″ × 108″

PAPER PIECING

- Foundation paper (You can use typing paper, specialty foundation piecing paper—such as Carol Doak's Foundation Paper—or even newsprint, but be careful using any paper with ink that might rub off.)

- Fabric gluestick

SPECIAL TOOLS (OPTIONAL)

- Fons & Porter Half and Quarter Ruler

CUTTING

If you need help with cutting, take a look at Cutting (page 25).

SCRAPS

- Cut a lot of strips. Try to cut strips no less than 1½″ wide; smaller than that and they become too narrow for piecing. Anything wider than 3″ is getting too thick; you want each star point to have plenty of variety.

WEDGWOOD BLUE

- Cut 30 strips 7″ × width of fabric; subcut into 360 rectangles 3½″ × 7″.

- Cut 45 squares 10½″ × 10½″ for setting squares.

DOTTED BLACK

- *If using optional ruler,** cut 10 strips 3½″ × width of fabric; subcut into 180 half-square triangles.
  Otherwise, cut 9 strips 4″ × width of fabric; subcut into 90 squares 4″ × 4″ and cut each square in half diagonally to yield 180 half-square triangles.

BINDING

- Cut 10 strips 2½″ × width of fabric.

* Fons & Porter Half and Quarter Ruler

Bed is the poor man's opera.

ITALIAN PROVERB

CONSTRUCTION

If you need help with construction, take a look at Construction Basics (page 24). Seam allowances are ¼".

STAR BLOCKS

1. Copy the foundation-piecing pattern (page 88) onto foundation paper. Make 180 copies.

2. Join string scraps to create panels that are roughly 8" × 20". Make 26 panels.

String panel; make 26.

> ### TIP
> Strips from fat quarters will work just fine in the 8" × 20" panels.

3. Cut 180 triangular chunks from the panels (7 from each panel). These don't have to be precise, just large enough to cover the triangle on the foundation paper. Cut at different angles for more variety in the chunks and to get the most from each panel.

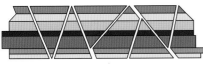

Cut chunks to cover triangle.

> ### TIP
> Think of it this way: the lines are on the *back* of the paper. They are what you will be looking at as you sew. It could be said that with paper piecing, you are building a block from the back.

4. Swipe a bit of glue on the front of the paper in Section 1. Place a chunk of string piecing that you cut in Step 2 so it completely covers Section 1.

Place string piecing on Section 1.

5. Place a Wedgwood blue rectangle so it will cover Section 2. Then flip over the blue rectangle so it is right sides together with the string piecing. The Section 2 rectangle needs to be placed so that there will be about a ¼" seam allowance hanging over the sewing line.

Place blue rectangle to cover Section 2.

Flip over blue fabric so it is right sides together with string piecing.

> ### TIPS
> • To make sure each piece of fabric will cover the appropriate section, pin along the sewing line before sewing and flip the fabric over to make sure the section is covered and there are adequate seam allowances.
>
> • Shorten the stitch length to about 2.0. Using a shorter stitch will make it easier when you tear off the paper after the stitching is done.

6. Use a pin to hold the pieces in place. Flip over the fabric and paper and sew on the line between Section 1 and Section 2.

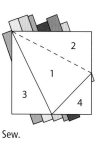

Sew.

7. Press back the blue rectangle. The piece should completely cover the Section 2 triangle on the foundation paper. If it doesn't, rip out the seam and try again. You'll get the hang of it—promise! Once the piece is sewn properly, fold back paper at the seam and trim the seam allowance to ¼″.

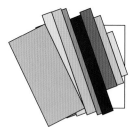

Press back blue rectangle.

8. Continue sewing on the paper. Add the second blue rectangle and then the black center.

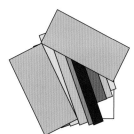 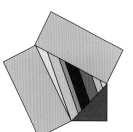

Add second blue rectangle.   Add black center.

TIP

You may want to do the string piecing on paper, too. It's not necessary, but some piecers like the stability paper gives them when handling all those long, loose scraps.

---

9. When all the blocks are sewn, use the lines on the paper to trim them with a rotary cutter and ruler to 5½″ × 5½″ square. Ta-da! You've got a quadrant.

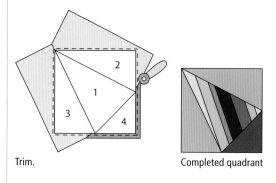

Trim.   Completed quadrant

10. Join 4 block quadrants to complete 1 block. Press the seams in alternate directions so the seams nest when the quadrants are sewn together. Make 45 blocks.

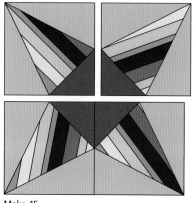

Make 45.

QUILT ASSEMBLY

Take a look at the quilt photo (page 82) and the quilt assembly diagram (page 88).

Sew together the blocks into rows, alternating the Star blocks with the setting blocks. Press the seams in alternate directions so they nest when the rows are sewn together. Sew together the rows.

FINISHING

If you need help with finishing, take a look at Putting Together the Layers (page 33) and Finishing Up (page 35).

1. Sew together yardage or scraps as needed to make the backing 4″–10″ bigger on all sides than the quilt top.

2. Layer the backing, batting, and quilt top. Baste and quilt as you please.

3. Create French fold binding in white/black fabric. Sew the binding to the quilt.

4. Obtain ice cream. Go back to bed.

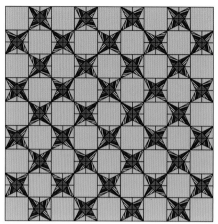

Quilt assembly

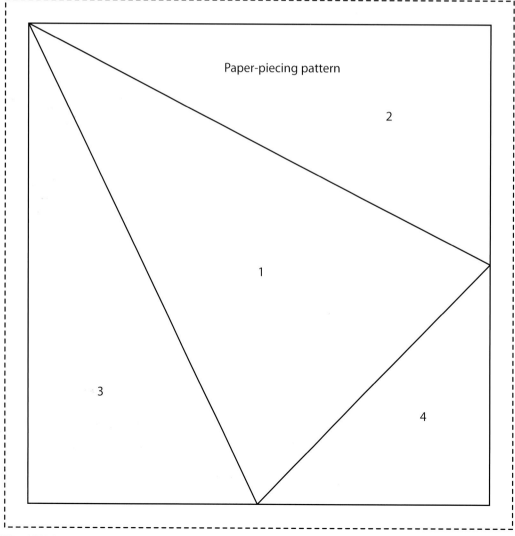

Paper-piecing pattern

2

1

3

4

B-SIDE

My second favorite ice cream flavor is pistachio. So green had to make an appearance.

Rum Raisin
2018
Mary fons
"Every fibre of her frame"

Quilt Charm

QUILTING MEMO

Bubbles, bubbles everywhere. Or plump raisins? Either way, it's sweet.

HERZOG

MADE BY MARY FONS, QUILTED BY LUANN DOWNS

Finished quilt: 100″ × 100″   Finished block: 32″ × 32″

I read for at least an hour every day before the sun comes up. One of my favorite writers is Saul Bellow, a giant of twentieth-century literature. His writing is basically perfect: clean, shocking, true, hilarious, and heart-wrenching, page after page after page.

I was reading *Herzog* (the book) around the time I began making *Herzog* (the quilt). Although Bellow's novel isn't exactly a love story, it's not *not* a love story, either; so I figured the quilt would be at home in this book. The scale of this quilt is huge, like the cities where *Herzog* is set (Chicago and New York), and the dark colors feel very male.

This quilt is a beast. It's really big. When you eventually join rows, watch for drag at the machine. I recommend rolling up the side of the top not being sewn and putting it up over your shoulder. Making a quilt, much like living life, is a total-body process.

MATERIALS

BLOCKS

- 2 yards brown linen
- ⅝ yard each of 4 different purples, maroons, and/or lavenders

  Note: Each large Thousand Waves block (the big X blocks) uses 1 purple throughout. Mixing them all up could work, but there's more visual interest if each X is distinctly different from the others.

- 6 fat quarters or 4 cuts ⅓ yard each of assorted pale or light yellows

SASHING

- 1 yard salmon

ALTERNATE BLOCKS

- 4⅝ yards solid black

BACKING

- 9 yards total scraps or yardage

BINDING

- ⅞ yard solid black

BATTING

- 108″ × 108″

SPECIAL TOOLS (OPTIONAL)

- Fons & Porter Half and Quarter Ruler

CUTTING

If you need help with cutting, take a look at Cutting (page 25).

BROWN

- *If using optional ruler,** cut 12 strips 4½″ × width of fabric; subcut into 192 half-square triangles.

  Otherwise, cut 12 strips 4⅞″ × width of fabric; subcut into 96 squares; cut each square in half diagonally to yield 192 half-square triangles.

  * Fons & Porter Half and Quarter Ruler

PURPLES

From each purple:

- *If using optional ruler,** cut 3 strips 4½″ × width of fabric; subcut into 48 half-square triangles.

  Otherwise, cut 3 strips 4⅞″ × width of fabric; subcut into 24 squares; cut each square in half diagonally to yield 48 half-square triangles.

  With either method, there will be a total of 192 purple half-square triangles.

YELLOWS

- *If using optional ruler**:

  If using 6 fat quarters: From each fat quarter, cut 4 strips 4½″ × short width of fat quarter; subcut into 12 half-square triangles and 6 squares 4½″ × 4½″.

  If using ⅓-yard cuts of fabric: Cut 2 strips 4½″ × width of fabric; subcut into 16 half-square triangles and 8 squares 4½″ × 4½″.

CUTTING LARGE SQUARES

Cutting large squares accurately can be challenging. You can do the math, make precise folds, slice, and then end up with a piece of fabric that is large and lovely … and *almost* square. To be safe and accurate, I use a pair of yardsticks or a T-square to mark out what I need on my yardage using a fabric marking pen or pencil. Then I get out my fabric scissors and cut out my large square carefully. Always cut with the grain. A square cut on the bias will stay square for about two seconds.

YELLOWS (CONTINUED)

* *Without optional ruler:*

  If using 6 fat quarters: From each fat quarter, cut 2 strips 4⅞″ × shorter width of fat quarter; subcut into 6 squares, cut each square in half diagonally to yield 12 half-square triangles. Cut 2 strips 4½″ × short width of fat quarter; subcut into 6 squares 4½″ × 4½″.

  If using ⅓-yard cuts of fabric: Cut 1 strip 4⅞″ × width of fabric; subcut into 8 squares 4⅞″ × 4⅞″; cut each square in half diagonally to yield 16 half-square triangles. Cut 1 strip 4½″ × width of fabric; subcut into 8 squares 4½″ × 4½″.

SALMON

* Cut 8 sashing A strips 2½″ × 32½″.

* Cut 4 sashing B strips 2½″ × 34½″.

BLACK

* Cut 5 squares 32½″ × 32½″.

BINDING

* Cut 11 strips 2½″ × width of fabric for binding.

> In expressing love, we belong among the undeveloped countries.
>
> SAUL BELLOW

CONSTRUCTION

If you need help with construction, take a look at Construction Basics (page 24). Seam allowances are ¼″.

JUMBO X BLOCKS

1. Sew together half-square triangles. Make 40 brown and purple, 8 purple and yellow, and 8 brown and yellow.

Make half-square triangle units.

2. Sew together the half-square triangle units into quadrants, pressing the seams in each row in alternate directions so they nest when the rows are sewn together. Sew together the quadrants to make a complete block. Repeat to make the other 3 jumbo X blocks.

Make quadrants.

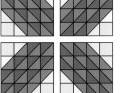
Make 4 blocks.

QUILT ASSEMBLY

Take a look at the quilt photo (page 90) and the quilt assembly diagram (below).

1. Sew together the blocks and sashing A strips into rows.

2. Sew 2 strips of 2 sashing B and 1 sashing A end to end.

3. Sew the 3 block rows together with these long sashing strips between them.

FINISHING

If you need help with finishing, take a look at Putting Together the Layers (page 33) and Finishing Up (page 35).

1. Sew together yardage or scraps as needed to make the backing 4″–10″ bigger on all sides than the quilt top.

2. Layer backing, batting, and quilt top. Baste and quilt as you please.

3. Create French fold binding in black fabric. Sew the binding to the quilt.

4. Settle in with a good book.

Quilt Charm

TIP

With so much negative space in the black portions, you've got an almost distressing number of options for quilting. I had a professional longarm quilter take this one on; I selected big, free-form flowers to hint at *Herzog's* feminine side.

Other options could include text from the book, circles (the character goes around and around in them), or straight lines like notebook paper.

B-SIDE

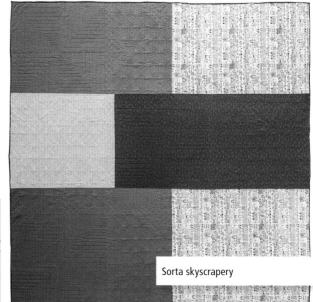

Sorta skyscrapery

QUILTING MEMO

I work with talented longarm quilters ... and that has made all the difference.

MY DEAR

MADE BY MARY FONS

Finished quilt: 90″ × 102″   Finished unit: 9″ × 9″, 12″ × 12″

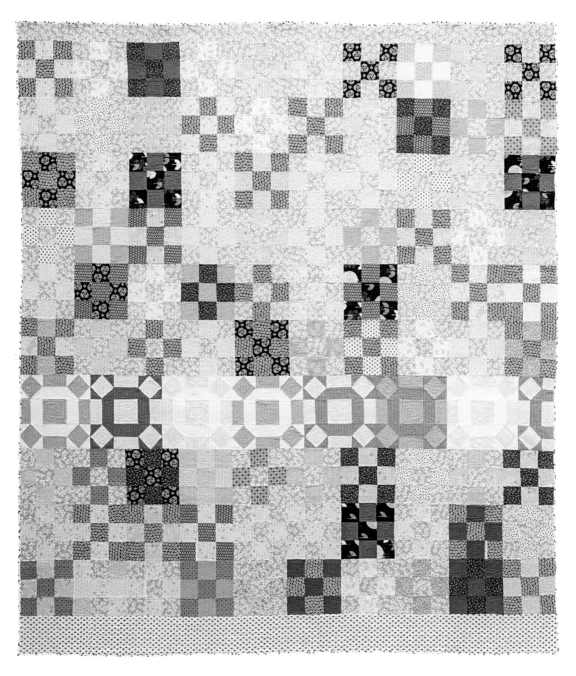

It's incredible how well-suited traditional quilts are to modern home decor. This quilt—shabby chic, even chintzy—looks great on black leather mid-century furniture. I know because I tried it.

The fizzy, floral Nine-Patches tossed together might run amok if the parade of Rolling Stones didn't march in and calm everything down. The rogue blocks here become the focus.

Perhaps a line of a different block would please you; go for it. I promise: Other traditional blocks, such as the Sawtooth Star or Grandmother's Fan, will work just as well and never go out of style.

MATERIALS

BLOCKS AND TOP BORDER

- 2¾ yards light blue-and-white floral print

- 2 yards total assorted patterned pink florals (for Nine-Patch blocks)

- ½-yard cuts of at least 6 different patterned pinks, blues, purples, navies, and grays (for Nine-Patch blocks)

- ½ yard each of 2 shades of pink linen

- 1 yard total assorted solids (minimum ⅛ yard for each Rolling Stone block)

BOTTOM BORDER

- ¾ yard black-and-white shirting print

BACKING

- 8⅜ yards total scraps or yardage

BINDING

- ⅞ yard black

BATTING

- 98″ × 110″

FABRIC NOTE

This quilt uses the same concept as patterned neutrals (page 16), but with more color. The effect of the pinks, blues, purples, and grays is what I would consider shabby chic. I didn't let the number of fabrics go too far, though: I don't believe there are more than ten different prints here; more would take it into the realm of messy. Remember: with great scrappy power comes great scrappy responsibility.

CUTTING

If you need help with cutting, take a look at Cutting (page 25).

BLUE-AND-WHITE PRINT

- Cut 22 strips 3½″ × width of fabric; subcut into 260 squares 3½″ × 3½″.

- Cut 3 pieces 3½″ × width of fabric for top border.

PATTERNED PINK FLORAL AND ASSORTED PATTERNED PRINTS

- Cut 46 strips 3½″ × width of fabric; subcut into 550 squares 3½″ × 3½″.

PINK LINEN

- From each shade of linen, cut 6 strips 2½″ × width of fabric; subcut into 64 B squares 2½″ × 2½″. The 2 remaining strips of each color will be used in strip sets.

ASSORTED SOLID FABRICS (FOR ROLLING STONE BLOCKS)

- For each of the 8 blocks, cut 1 strip 4½″ × width of fabric; subcut into 5 A squares 4½″ × 4½″; trim the remaining 4½″-wide fabric strip to 2½″ wide for strip set.

BLACK-AND-WHITE SHIRTING

- Cut 3 pieces 6½″ × width of fabric for bottom border.

BINDING

- Cut 11 strips 2½″ × width of fabric.

CONSTRUCTION

If you need help with construction, take a look at Construction Basics (page 24). Seam allowances are ¼".

NINE-PATCH BLOCKS

Sew together the 3½" × 3½" squares into rows of 3. Press the seams toward the darker fabric. Sew together the rows into Nine-Patches. Make 90 blocks.

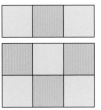

Make 90.

TIP

For the most part, I kept the slightly darker print in each block on the "outside." It seemed to ground the blocks in a subtle way.

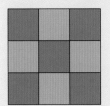

Darker squares on the outside

ROLLING STONE BLOCKS

1. Make the Rolling Stone blocks using what I call the "flippy corner" method: Place a pink B square on the corner of a solid A square, right sides together. If you like, you can draw a sewing line from corner to corner before you stitch.

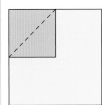

With right sides together, sew diagonal seam.

2. Trim the excess to a ¼" seam allowance and press open to reveal the triangle corner. Repeat for remaining corners to complete the unit. Make 32 units.

Trim excess.   Press back to reveal triangle.

Completed flippy corner unit

3. Create strip sets by sewing together a 2½″-wide pink strip and a solid strip. From the strip sets, cut 4 squares 4½″ × 4½″ for each block, 32 total.

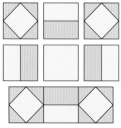

Make strip sets and cut squares.   ⊢— 4½ —⊣

4. Arrange the units of the block, including the solid square in the center. Sew together the units into rows and press the seams in alternate directions so they nest when the rows are sewn together. Sew together the rows to complete the block. Make 7 blocks plus 1 half-block. You can piece a half-block, or sew a full block, fold it in half, lightly crease it, then cut ¼″ away from the crease.

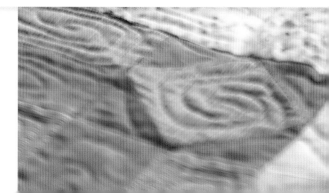

Make 7 blocks and 1 half-block.

The finest souls are those that have the most variety and suppleness.

MICHEL DE MONTAIGNE

QUILT ASSEMBLY

Take a look at the quilt photo (page 96) and the quilt assembly diagram (below).

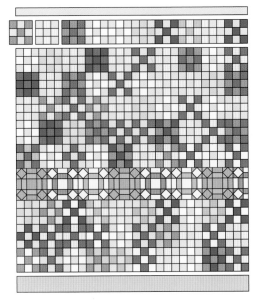

1. Sew together the 16″-wide pieces for the pillow space. You can cut the 3 pieces to 30½″ and then sew them together, or just sew the 3 width-of-fabric pieces together and then trim the unit to 90½″.

2. Sew together the 11″-wide pieces for the bottom border.

3. Sew together the blocks into rows. Press the seams in alternate directions so they nest when the rows are sewn together. Sew together the rows.

4. Sew the top border/pillow space to the top of the quilt top (take a look at Borders, page 33, as needed). Sew the bottom border to the bottom of the quilt top.

FINISHING

If you need help with finishing, take a look at Putting Together the Layers (page 33) and Finishing Up (page 35).

1. Sew together yardage or scraps as needed to make the backing 4″–10″ bigger on all sides than the quilt top.

2. Layer backing, batting, and quilt top. Baste and quilt as you please.

3. Create French fold binding in black fabric. Sew the binding to the quilt.

4. Take a nap, for heaven's sake!

> **TIP**
>
> I suggest not laboring much over the quilting on this quilt because it won't show up. The patterns are so busy, the quilting takes a back seat. Save intricate quilting for a work with more negative space.

B-SIDE

Because the top of this quilt was so unabashedly girly, I gave it some grown-up black on the back. I love the combination of flirty and serious.

Quilt Charm

QUILTING MEMO

As if it weren't sweet enough, this quilt called for a swirl in each square— think cinnamon roll.

DEVOTEE

MADE BY MARY FONS, QUILTED BY SALLY EVANSHANK

Finished quilt: 74″ × 90″   Finished block: 8″ × 8″

DEVOTEE:

(de•voh•TEE; *noun*) a person who is very interested in and enthusiastic about someone or something; for example: *I am a devotee of gorgeous fabric.*

This quilt is unique in that I used only four fabrics to make it. The intense pattern in the red print and the thinness of the strips themselves create all the movement needed—drawing the eye anywhere else would be too much.

Are you a devotee? In what (or whom) are you interested and enthusiastic? I'm a big fan of both interest *and* enthusiasm; you might say I'm devoted to both concepts.

MATERIALS

BLOCKS AND BORDERS

- 2⅛ yards tomato red print
- 1½ yards light green
- 3¼ yards light denim* blue
- 2¾ yards snow white or lightly printed white

BACKING

- 5½ yards total scraps or yardage

BATTING

- 82″ × 98″

BINDING

- ¾ yard white

PAPER PIECING

- Fabric gluestick
- Foundation paper (You can use typing paper, specialty foundation piecing paper—such as Carol Doak's Foundation Paper—or even newsprint, but be careful using any paper with ink that might rub off, especially because you're using snow white fabric.)

* *I say "denim," but I don't mean actual denim, of course. I found a quilter's linen at the old Vogue Fabrics store near my home in Chicago and fell in love. It looks like blue jeans.*

CUTTING

If you need help with cutting, take a look at Cutting (page 25).

RED, GREEN, AND BLUE

- Cut approximately 46 strips 1½″ × width of fabric from red.
- Cut approximately 31 strips 1½″ × width of fabric from green.
- Cut approximately 72 strips 1½″ × width of fabric from blue; 8 strips are for inner border.

> **TIP**
>
> I suggest cutting in batches. Cut a third of what you need, then sew. This is because you're essentially cutting the fabric into ribbons. Most of us will end up pulling from spaghetti-like piles, and few of us are keen on the idea of re-ironing anything, especially long, skinny strips. Working in smaller batches will reduce the likelihood that you'll need to re-press before you make the blocks.

WHITE

- Cut 14 strips 3½″ × width of fabric; subcut into 160 squares 3½″ × 3½″ for corners of blocks.
- Cut 8 strips 4½″ × width of fabric for outer border.
- Cut 9 strips 2½″ × width of fabric for binding.

What else is love but understanding and rejoicing in the fact that another person lives, acts, and experiences otherwise than we do?

FRIEDRICH NIETZSCHE

CONSTRUCTION

If you need help with construction, take a look at Construction Basics (page 24). Seam allowances are ¼".

PAPER-PIECED BLOCKS

Important: Shorten the stitch length on your machine. I find a 2.0mm stitch is about right for paper piecing like this. Shorter stitches make it easier to rip off the paper from the block when it's all done, and the stitch will remain strong after all that tugging.

1. Cut 80 pieces of foundation paper to 8½" × 8½".

2. Place a blue strip right side up diagonally across the middle of a foundation paper. Trim the excess fabric. It's helpful to use a dot of fabric glue to hold this first strip in place.

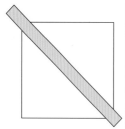

Place first strip right side up.

3. Place a red strip facedown on top of the first blue strip and sew it down.

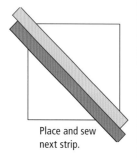

Place and sew next strip.

4. Press the strip open. Repeat with another strip of red on the other side of the first blue strip.

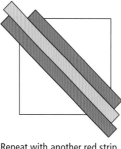

Repeat with another red strip.

5. Keep going, alternating colors until you get 3 blue and 4 red strips in the block.

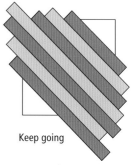

Keep going

6. Place a white square facedown on each side of the last red strip. Stitch along the diagonal and press the pieces open.

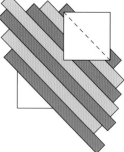

Add white squares.

7. Place the block paper side up on a cutting mat and trim so the fabric is even with the paper.

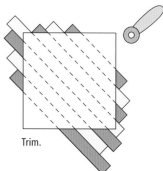

Trim.

8. Gently tear off the paper from the back of the block. Make a total of 48 of these blue and red blocks.

Make 48.

9. Create 32 green and blue blocks in the same manner as steps 1–8.

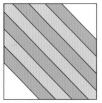

Make 32.

BORDERS

1. For the inner border, join 7 blue 1½″ strips end to end.

2. For the outer border, join the 8 white 4½″ strips end to end.

QUILT ASSEMBLY

Take a look at the quilt photo (page 104) and the quilt assembly diagram (below).

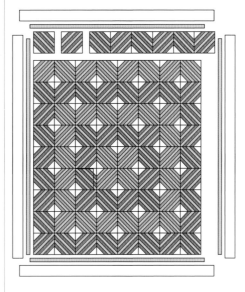

1. Sew together the blocks into rows. Press the seams in alternate directions so they nest when the rows are sewn together. Sew together the rows.

2. Measure the length of the quilt top and cut 2 blue inner side borders this length. Sew the side borders to the quilt top and press the seams toward the border. Measure the width of the quilt and cut the blue inner top and bottom borders this length. Sew them to the quilt and press the seams toward the border. Repeat this process for the outer white border.

FINISHING

If you need help with finishing, take a look at Putting Together the Layers (page 33) and Finishing Up (page 35).

1. Sew together yardage or scraps as needed to make the backing 4″–10″ bigger on all sides than the quilt top.

2. Layer the backing, batting, and quilt top. Baste and quilt as you please.

3. Create French fold binding in black fabric. Sew the binding to the quilt.

4. Enjoy, enthusiastically.

B-SIDE

A moment of serenity after all that action on the top …

Quilt Charm

QUILTING MEMO

I love, love, love a grid in a quilt. It's the quintessential "quilted" look. Perfect.

NIGHT SKY

MADE BY MARY FONS, QUILTED BY EBONY LOVE

Finished quilt: 97½″ × 129½″   Finished block: 7½″ × 7½″

While making this quilt I was working on my master's degree, taking a course in cosmology. I spent a lot of time looking at the sky at night and at pictures of deep, dark space. Did you know our galaxy is just one of *500 billion* galaxies in the universe? Just think: There might actually be more fabric on other planets.

In *Night Sky*, low-contrast blocks set the stage for the rogue blocks—the stars—to catch your attention. The goal is muted, not somber or sad, so the caramel and chocolate sashing makes sure this quilt stays out of the dark.

MATERIALS

BLOCKS

- 7⅝ yards solid black for background
- 1 yard assorted greige (a color between beige and gray)
- 1 yard assorted slate gray
- ¾ yard patterned deep gray or patterned black
- 1 fat quarter crimson rogue prints
- 2 fat quarters vanilla rogue prints (page 23)
- 2 fat quarters other rogue prints (blue and green in mine)

SASHING

- 1¾ yards caramel linen for vertical sashing and edges
- 1⅜ yards chocolate linen for horizontal sashing

BACKING

- 11½ yards total scraps or yardage

BATTING

- 106″ × 138″

BINDING

- ⅞ yard black

SPECIAL TOOLS (OPTIONAL)

- Fons & Porter Half and Quarter Ruler

CUTTING

If you need help with cutting, take a look at Cutting (page 25).

BLACK

- *If using optional ruler,** cut 22 strips 3½″ × width of fabric; subcut into 396 half-square triangles.
  Otherwise, cut 20 strips 3⅞″ × width of fabric; subcut into 198 squares; cut each square in half diagonally to yield 396 half-square triangles.
- Cut 8 strips 8″ × width of fabric for bottom and side borders.
- Cut 3 strips 22″ × width of fabric for top border / pillow space.
- Cut 24 strips 2″ × width of fabric; from the strips cut 495 A squares 2″ × 2″.

GREIGE, GRAYS, PATTERNED BLACKS, AND ROGUES

- *If using optional ruler,** cut 22 strips 3½″ × width of fabric, including 1 or 2 strips from each fat quarter; subcut into 396 half-square triangles.
  Otherwise, cut 20 strips 3⅞″ × width of fabric, including 1 or 2 strips from each fat quarter; subcut into 198 squares and cut each in half diagonally to yield 396 half-square triangles.
- Cut 25 strips 2″ × width of fabric, including 1 or 2 strips from each fat quarter; subcut into 396 B squares 2″ × 2″ for blocks and 120 squares 2″ × 2″ for cornerstones (516 squares total).

CARAMEL LINEN

- Cut 7 strips 8″ × width of fabric; from the strips cut 128 rectangles 2″ × 8″ for sashing.

CHOCOLATE LINEN

- Cut 5 strips 8″ × width of fabric; from the strips cut 90 rectangles 2″ × 8″ for sashing.

BINDING

- Cut 12 strips 2½″ × width of fabric.

* *Fons & Porter Half and Quarter Ruler*

CONSTRUCTION

If you need help with construction, take a look at Construction Bascis (page 24). Seam allowances are ¼".

1. Sew together half-square triangles to complete 4 half-square triangle units.

Sew together triangles.

2. Sew together A squares and B squares to make 4 A/B units.

Sew together squares.

3. Sew together units with an A square to make a Churn Dash block, as shown. Press the seams in each row in opposite directions so they'll nest. Repeat to make a total of 99 blocks.

Churn Dash block; make 99.

4. Sew a cornerstone to 119 of the caramel sashing strips.

Add cornerstone to sashing strip.

QUILT ASSEMBLY

Take a look at the quilt photo (page 112) and the quilt assembly diagram (below).

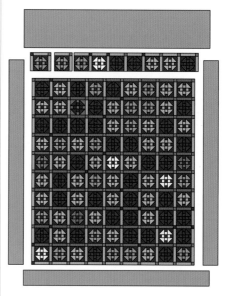

1. Arrange all the blocks on a design wall or on the floor. After you have decided on the arrangement, sew the sashing to the blocks, noting the placement of the caramel and chocolate strips. Refer to the quilt assembly diagram for sashing placement, noting that the first block in each row will have 3 sashing pieces sewn on, and the remaining blocks in that row will have 2 sashing pieces sewn on.

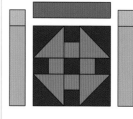
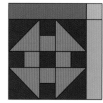

Add sashing to blocks.

2. Sew together the blocks into rows. Press the seams in alternate directions so they nest when the rows are sewn together. Sew together the rows, adding the bottom sashing strips and final cornerstone.

3. Sew together the 8″-wide border strips for length. Measure the quilt, cut, and sew on the side borders as described in Borders (page 33).

4. The remaining 8″-wide border is for the bottom. Measure, cut, and sew on the bottom border.

5. For 22″-wide top border/pillow space, sew together the 22″-wide strips to make the border wide enough for the quilt. Measure, cut, and sew on the top border.

FINISHING

If you need help with finishing, take a look at Putting Together the Layers (page 33) and Finishing Up (page 35).

1. Sew together yardage or scraps as needed to make the backing 4″–10″ bigger on all sides than the quilt top.

2. Layer backing, batting, and quilt top. Baste and quilt as you please.

3. Create French fold binding in black fabric. Sew the binding to the quilt.

4. Stargaze.

> **TIP**
>
> As you place rogue blocks, check distribution frequently. If you choose not to replicate my placement exactly, you'll rearrange many times, so keep looking up at your design wall and playing musical chairs with the blocks.

I don't say we all ought to misbehave, but we ought to look as if we could.

ORSON WELLES

B-SIDE

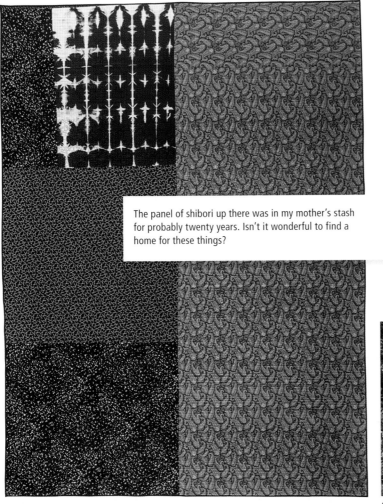

The panel of shibori up there was in my mother's stash for probably twenty years. Isn't it wonderful to find a home for these things?

Night Sky
2013
Mary Fons
Judge not

Quilt Charm

QUILTING MEMO

From the sky to the ground: Pebbles in rows, alternating off and on, were a way to bring variety and ground the stars (in a good way).

EMBERS

MADE BY MARY FONS, QUILTED BY RUTHMARY SCHAUER

Finished quilt: 80″ × 105″   Finished blocks: 7″ × 7″, 14″ × 14″

Curling up under a quilt in front of a roaring fire is a universally appealing idea: Humans have been snuggling together to smooch and dream and gaze at a crackling fire for thousands of years. This quilt makes use of patterned neutrals in the border and on the corners of the red snowballs (Are they coals?) as well. The intended effect is one of warmth, complexity, and utter uniqueness, like any good fire—or good person—you encounter.

MATERIALS

BLOCKS AND BORDERS

- 3¼ yards total scrappy ruby reds and magentas
- 3 yards patterned neutrals in blacks, grays, and deep browns
- ⅛ yard gingham black
- 1¼ yards tan for border
- 3¼ yards solid black for sashing and large top and bottom blocks

BACKING

- 7½ yards total scraps or yardage

BATTING

- 88″ × 113″

BINDING

- ⅞ yard solid black

It's not true that I had nothing on. I had the radio on.

MARILYN MONROE

CUTTING

If you need help with cutting, take a look at Cutting (page 25).

SCRAPPY REDS

- Cut 31 strips 4″ × width of fabric; subcut into 304 squares 4″ × 4″. These are the A squares.
- Cut 2 squares 7½″ × 7½″.

PATTERNED BLACKS, GRAYS, BROWNS, AND GINGHAM

- Cut 44 strips 1½″ × width of fabric; subcut into 1,216 squares 1½″ × 1½″. These are the B squares.
- Cut 4 strips 8¼″ × width of fabric; subcut into 19 squares 8¼″ × 8¼″.
- Cut 1 strip 2¼″ × width of fabric; subcut into 8 squares 2¼″ × 2¼″.

TAN

- Cut 4 strips 8¼″ × width of fabric; subcut into 19 squares 8¼″ × 8¼″.

SOLID BLACK

- Cut 2 strips 14½″ × width of fabric; subcut into 20 rectangles 14½″ × 2½″.
- Cut 3 strips 16½″ × width of fabric; subcut into 2 squares 16½″ × 16½″ and 26 rectangles 16½″ × 2½″.
- Cut 1 strip 24½″ × width of fabric; subcut into 2 rectangles 24½″ × 16½″.
- Cut 1 strip 2½″ × width of fabric; subcut into 2 rectangles 2½″ × 18½″.

BINDING

- Cut 10 strips 2½″ × length of fabric.

CONSTRUCTION

If you need help with construction, take a look at Construction Basics (page 24). Seam allowances are ¼".

SNOWBALL BLOCKS

1. Make the red Snowball blocks using the "flippy corner" method. Place a black, brown, or gray B square on the corners of a red A square, right sides together. If you like, you can draw a sewing line from corner to corner before you stitch. Sew the diagonal seam.

2. Trim the seam allowances to ¼" and press open to reveal the triangle corner. Make 304 blocks with the 4" squares and 2 with the 7" squares.

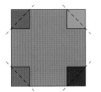

With right sides together, sew diagonal seams.

3. Put together the quilt in large sections of 16 blocks.

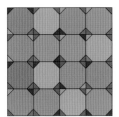

Sew together 16 blocks.

4. Sew 2 sashing strips to each of 10 large blocks—1 strip 14½" long and 1 strip 16½" long.

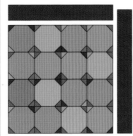

Sew sashing to 2 sides of 10 large blocks.

5. Sew 3 sashing strips to each of 8 large blocks—1 strip 14½" long and 2 strips 16½" long.

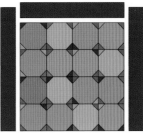

Sew sashing to 3 sides of 8 large blocks.

6. Sew 4 sashing strips to 1 large block—2 strips 14½" long and 2 strips 18½" long.

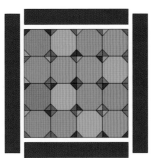

Sew sashing to 4 sides of 1 large block.

BORDER HOURGLASS BLOCKS

Sew the tan and black/brown Hourglass blocks, following the method in Hourglass Units (page 64, in *The Royal We*), substituting the tan square for the white square, and the black/brown square for the solid black square. Make 38 Hourglass blocks.

QUILT ASSEMBLY

Take a look at the quilt photo (page 120) and the quilt assembly diagram (next column).

1. Sew together the blocks into rows, adding solid black blocks to the first and last rows. Press the seams in alternate directions so they nest when the rows are sewn together. Sew together the rows.

Blocks with sashing

2. Sew 10 Hourglass blocks together for the bottom border. Center the border on the bottom of the quilt (it will be longer than the quilt) and pin in place. Sew the border to the quilt and trim the ends even with the sides of the quilt.

3. Sew 14 Hourglass blocks together and one 7½˝ Snowball block at the end. Repeat for the other side border. Sew the side borders to the quilt.

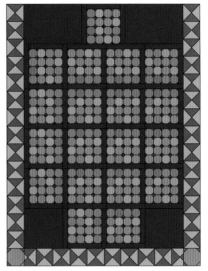

Quilt assembly

FINISHING

If you need help with finishing, take a look at Putting Together the Layers (page 33) and Finishing Up (page 35).

1. Sew together yardage or scraps as needed to make the backing 4˝–10˝ bigger on all sides than the quilt top.

2. Layer the backing, batting, and quilt top. Baste and quilt as you please.

3. Create French fold binding in black fabric. Sew the binding to the quilt.

4. Start a fire.

B-SIDE

I had a tiny checkerboard leftover and a vintage piece of this crazy Aspen snowbunny fabric from the 1970s. It made me think of playing games after hitting the slopes, perfect for the back of a quilt called *Embers*.

Embers
2013
Mary Fons
"Postmen like doctors"

Quilt Charm

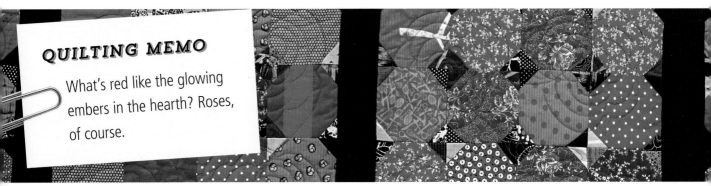

QUILTING MEMO

What's red like the glowing embers in the hearth? Roses, of course.

ABOUT THE AUTHOR

Mary Fons is a writer and performer who currently works in the quilt industry. Prior to entering the family business, she was a full-time freelance writer (How Stuff Works, Jellyvision, Publications International, Soft Skull Press, and others) and stage performer (Neo-Futurist ensemble 2006–2012, Gift Theater Co. founding member) in Chicago. Her work as a poet can be read in *Learn Then Burn: A Poetry Anthology for the Classroom* (Write Bloody) and *Slam Poetry for Dummies* (Alpha Books), and many of her poems can be found on YouTube. Mary continues to perform original work at live-lit events across Chicago, the best city on the planet. She was born in Iowa.

In 2010, she created *Quilty* (New Track Media), a weekly online program she hosts for beginner quilters. She now serves as editor and creative director of *Quilty* magazine, available bimonthly on fine newsstands nationwide and via digital subscription. Since 2011, Mary has served as co-host of *Love of Quilting* on PBS/Create Network alongside her mother, quilter and educator Marianne Fons.

Mary's quilts are frequently featured in *Love of Quilting* and *Quilty* magazines. She lectures widely and her popular blog, PaperGirl, can be found at maryfons.com. For more about Mary, Quilt Charms, or to inquire about workshops and lectures, visit maryfons.com.

RESOURCES

Color reference tools

Pantone LLC   pantone.com

Quilting books from C&T Publishing

Beginner's Guide to Free-Motion Quilting by Natalia Bonner

First Steps to Free-Motion Quilting by Christina Cameli

Get Addicted to Free-Motion Quilting by Sheila Sinclair Snyder

In the Studio with Angela Walters by Angela Walters

Modern Quilting Designs by Bethany Pease

Mary Fons booking, inquiries, and exclusive products

maryfons.com

Quilty online programs and information

heyquilty.com • shopquilty.com • qnntv.com

Information about *Love of Quilting* on PBS/Create Network and Fons & Porter publications and products

fonsandporter.com • quiltersclubofamerica.com